RISE UP & SHINE!

D0963963

RISE UP & SHINE!

My Secrets for Success in Career, Relationships, and Life

CRISTINA
SARALEGUI

A CELEBRA BOOK

Celebra
Published by the Penguin Group
Penguin Group (USA) LLC, 375 Hudson Street,
New York, New York 10014

USA | Canada | UK | Ireland | Australia | New Zealand | India | South Africa | China
penguin.com
A Penguin Random House Company

First published by Celebra,
a division of Penguin Group (USA) LLC

First Printing, November 2014

CELEBRA ENGLISH-LANGUAGE EDITION ISBN: 978-0-451-47096-6

THE LIBRARY OF CONGRESS HAS CATALOGED THE SPANISH-LANGUAGE EDITION OF THIS TITLE AS
FOLLOWS:

Saralegui, Cristina.
    Pa'rriba y pa'lante!: mis secretos para triunfar en tu carrera, tu relación y tu vida/
Cristina Saralegui.
    p. cm.
    ISBN 978-0-451-47097-3
    1. Women—Life skills guides. I. Title. II. Title: Pa'rriba y pa'lante!
    HQ1227.S337 2014
    646.7—dc23   2014023849

Printed in the United States of America
10 9 8 7 6 5 4 3 2 1

Set in Berling

To my three children, Titi, Stephanie, and Jon, thank you for the sweetest moments of my life.

Contents

Contents

RISE UP & SHINE!

Introduction

Throughout the years, I've often found the first thing I'm asked when I meet people is for personal advice. Whether it be from journalists conducting an interview to moms I meet at the mall, they all want to know the same things—how I managed to pursue a successful career while raising a family and maintaining a solid, enduring marriage; how to pick a long-lasting partner; how to ask for a raise. In essence, they want to know how to find happiness and success in their own lives. I try to offer some piece of advice that might be useful, but in those few minutes, I can barely even scratch the surface. To truly share the secrets that have helped me triumph in life, I would need more than just those few minutes. We'd need to sit down and chat for hours and have a real heart-to-heart. And so, this book was born.

There is no specific formula that will guarantee you success in life. For each of us, that road is unique and different, especially because everyone defines success according to their particular dreams and needs. For me, winning in life means not only having a successful and fulfilling career, but also raising a family, and now being able to enjoy quality time with my husband, children, and grandchildren. Because, at the end of the day, you can't hug a career—you need to be surrounded by your family and friends. The secret to living a complete and happy life lies in finding that essential balance between your personal and professional goals. It's definitely no easy task. To get to where I am today, I had to endure tremendous blows, setbacks, and heartaches. But instead of giving up with every fall, I picked myself up, held my head high, and continued to find the will to rise up and shine.

Although every woman defines success as something different, I do believe there are some basic rules that, when put into practice, can help you reach your dreams. To start, you will need what I like to call the two P's: passion and perseverance. Because nothing in life is guaranteed, you need to have a strong sense of passion and perseverance to help push you forward when you're ready to throw in the towel. No matter what happens, never give up. The trials and tribulations life throws our way are actually the best lessons we will ever have within our reach. Without these difficult experiences, we would never be able to evolve and move on to the next stages of our lives. You should never stop learning and dreaming.

We must also learn to teach and share what we've learned. One of the things that I feel is lacking among women is an open dialogue where we can share our experiences, triumphs, and setbacks, so that we might help one another forge clearer paths to success and happiness. We must be more supportive of one another and speak more openly. In these chapters, you will find two types of boxes that highlight what I hope we will achieve together: staying informed and maintaining open and honest communication.

The information contained in the boxes labeled *Knowledge Is Power* is designed to help inform you. Having a wealth of knowledge is a powerful arsenal. If you read or hear something that grabs your attention or sparks questions, look deeper into it and find the answers. We must never stop informing ourselves. On that note, sharing knowledge is just as essential and valuable as accumulating it. Doing so creates a sense of solidarity that all women across different cultures and generations need to succeed. Within the boxes labeled *Sharing the Truth*, you'll find tools to help build and strengthen these lines of communication.

When you come across this box, don't be put off if what you read makes you feel uncomfortable. We must learn to communicate and talk about our unspoken truths. With *Sharing the Truth*, I want to break the silence and discuss topics that are normally taboo so that we can understand what we're facing.

During the last few years, I have managed to return to my professional roots, informing my audience on important subjects to help improve their lives. *Rise Up & Shine!* is a continuation of this goal. I want to share my secrets and experiences in hopes of helping others find their voices. As far back as I can remember, I have had to fight tooth and nail to not be invisible. When I was growing up, women with dreams and ambitions were largely ignored and were almost equivalent to being invisible, because those things were considered respectable and fitting for only men to pursue. Today, that has greatly changed, but women have yet to completely shed this invisibility.

The publication of this book coincides with my thirtieth wedding anniversary and fiftieth workforce anniversary. My entire life comes down to what I have learned on my personal and professional paths. In these pages, my goal is to share the lessons that have helped me succeed in life to help you triumph in your own. I hope to establish the sincere, open, and no-holds-barred communication I have always shared with my audience. I don't want anyone to be invisible in this world. Everyone, both women and men, are worth their weight in gold. *Rise Up & Shine!* is dedicated to everyone out there who seeks to live the best life possible. Enjoy the journey!

The only way to lose
your fear is to rise up
and face it head-on.

PART ONE

Career

1

Never Depend on Anyone
100 Percent

Like most children, I depended on my parents as a young girl. My father provided for all of my needs. Yes, the truth is that I never lacked anything. However, when I was a child, whenever I asked my dad for money to buy a new blouse, he would take me over to my closet and say, "Look how jammed your closet is! You can't even fit any more clothes in there." He never seemed to understand why I wanted a new item of clothing, and I couldn't comprehend why I had to justify the purchase of a new garment. When I was about sixteen years old, this happened again, and I suddenly asked myself, "Why do I have to explain to this man how many blouses I have, or how I've worn them so often that my friends have seen them too many times, or that my cousin has twice as many shirts as I do?" This exchange planted the first seed of financial independence. I realized that, in order to buy the things I wanted, I would have to look for a job.

No sooner said than done. Shortly thereafter, I got my first job. In those days, here in Miami there was a department store named Jordan Marsh, and they employed me as a sales associate within the cosmetics department. The salary was based on commission, so competition was fierce. But I had an advantage: my exceptional complexion. Clients approached me curious to find out my beauty secret. They wanted my porcelain skin, and I, being neither foolish nor lazy, recommended that my customers buy the most expensive creams available so that I could earn a little extra money. I never again had to ask my father for money to buy what I wanted. This was a lesson that stayed with me for the rest of my life.

That little seed of economic independence continued growing in me. By the time I turned eighteen, even though I had a wealthy father, I held a full-time job while attending the university. When it came to how I wanted to spend my hard-earned money, I didn't have to answer to anyone. This was a major step in my life, and helped me navigate my way through what came next.

While I was studying at the university, my father fell into financial hardship and had to choose between paying for my college education or my brother's. I remember vividly what he told me; his words were a rude awakening that would change me forever. My father clearly explained that it was his duty to give an education to my brother over me because one day, he would be married and need to support his wife and family; whereas I would be supported by my husband. From that moment, I vowed that I would never rely on my father, a husband, or any man for money ever again. This was my turning point in life, and it unleashed a fierce sense of self that has defined who I am today.

Soon after, I stopped going to school, and since I was unable to finish my degree, I focused all my energy on work. At that time I had an internship at *Vanidades* magazine, the leading woman's service magazine in the U.S. and Latin America. This became my first full-time job as a journalist and, unknowingly, marked the start of my career.

At twenty-six, with a clear career path, I decided to move out of my parents' home to a small apartment with my youngest sister. The thought of a woman leaving home without being married was unacceptable to my father, but being fully independent was something I needed to accomplish. My sister returned to my parents' home six months later, but I didn't. Although I greatly missed living with my family, I decided to continue moving forward with my plans. I never depended on anyone financially again.

No Woman Should Depend on Anyone 100 Percent

What would you think of a man who depended 100 percent on someone else? Women and men are equal; however, women are raised to believe in certain rules that sometimes end up setting us back. Many parents still ingrain in their children the mentality that it is the man who ought to seek a career and secure his independence, and while our culture has progressed to the point where it's acceptable for women to do that as well, there is still an implicit understanding that, if a woman lands a good husband with a good job, that can be her ticket to economic stability. Nothing could be farther from the truth, not only because financial independence is vital to your own self-worth, but also because, given the ups and downs of today's global economy, both parents must work in order to provide the best of everything for their children, including a good education.

Knowledge Is Power

According to the Center for American Progress, in 2010, in almost two-thirds (63.9 percent) of families with children in the United States, women were either breadwinners or co-breadwinners.

Let's return to the issue at hand, that of being financially dependent, especially if you depend on your partner or spouse. Asking your husband for money to buy something, what's that about? It'll get you nowhere. Being financially independent is a goal I want you to set in your life if you haven't already. It's a piece of advice I never get tired of sharing. It's so important, that I made sure to communicate it to my daughters beginning when they were children, and I hope to help them pass this lesson on to my grandchildren as well. I'm tired of seeing divorced and widowed women who don't even know how to write a check. My two daughters are married with children, but they continue to develop their careers. No woman should depend on anyone one hundred percent. Financial independence equals freedom.

> *Financial independence equals freedom.*

The Real Prince Charming Is Your Financial Freedom

How many of us grew up watching movies or hearing fairy tales about Prince Charming arriving right in the nick of time to save the princess? These stories are nothing but that—fiction. The truth is, if you don't save yourself, no one will. With financial independence comes freedom and the confidence from knowing that you can depend on yourself 100 percent. That is your real Prince Charming—the knight in shining armor who can get you out of sticky situations and always give you peace of mind. There are many women who tolerate husbands who beat them, who are drunks, who don't love them, but these women don't leave because they lack the means to support themselves. And let's not even talk about what happens if they have children. They are stuck because of their lack of independence. What kind of life is that? And what kind of example is that for your children? If you don't know how to be self-sufficient, how are you going to provide your children with the necessary tools to take care of themselves?

SHARING THE TRUTH

Women not only have to be able to fend for ourselves, but we must also be able to fend for our children without our husband's help. The best kind of preparation is financial independence. It's difficult to think about it, but the reality is your husband may one day decide to leave you for another woman or he may die in an accident or from an illness. If you are suddenly single or widowed and you do not know how to make a living, you will not be the only one to starve, so will your children.

I know what I'm talking about. If I hadn't been financially independent, divorcing my first husband would've been much harder. When I realized things weren't working out, having a career and earning my own money helped me make the right decision. Money was no obstacle. With the pain and hardships that come with the end of a relationship, adding the burden of financial dependence is like adding the weight of an elephant onto your shoulders. If you lack money of your own, your decisions are governed by its absence, and that can then take you down roads that may not be in your best interests. My first marriage lasted almost eight years, and it took four to carefully plan my exit strategy so as not to lose custody of my daughter or my money, but I managed it. Without financial independence, I may have taken another road, or the same one but with many more difficulties.

Don't Put All Your Eggs in One Basket

This is another piece of advice I never tire of repeating because I follow it faithfully: Do not put all your eggs in one basket. If you do, what will happen if that basket breaks? You will lose everything. Likewise, if you depend on someone 100 percent and that person disappears from your life, you will also lose everything. Again, it's worth repeating: Do not rely solely on someone else for financial support. Make sure you have something to fall back on if one day your partner is no longer around. When you dedicate your time and work to more than one thing—putting your eggs in different baskets instead of all in one—if one falls through, you can turn to the rest to stay afloat and move on. In other words, if you lose a job, you can use your experience, skills, and professional network to find another one; or if you lose a partner, you can rise up and shine thanks to your financial freedom.

My dad was always a very adventurous man. He was constantly searching for and creating new business opportunities. He was never afraid to take the road less traveled and face new challenges, like when he took off to Saudi Arabia in the seventies to build new schools. With his undertakings, he made millions of dollars and, as quickly as he earned them, he went bankrupt and lost it all because he wasn't really interested in building an empire and stabilizing that wealth. What was important to my dad was being able to support his wife and children. He was an incredible breadwinner, but a poor administrator.

One of the most important things I learned by riding my father's roller coaster of winning and losing it all, then winning again, is that you should never ever put all your eggs in one basket. That is how I came to be known as the woman with sixteen jobs. I worked at a magazine while also doing radio and TV shows, and even translated pamphlets that explained how airplanes worked. If you put your mind to it, you will find a multitude of possibilities for realizing financial independence. For example, if you're a good pastry chef, start up your own cake business; if you're fluent in two languages, become a translator; if you're interested in real estate, take night classes and get your license. The solution is almost always within your grasp if you're willing to make the effort. The sacrifice of holding down more than one job is nothing when compared to the peace of mind you enjoy with financial independence. I'll say it again: No woman should ever depend on anyone 100 percent.

Learn How to Manage Your Finances

Part of becoming financially independent is learning how to understand and manage your money. In many homes, the man is the one who handles the finances, so if he disappears, his partner or wife is suddenly left out in the cold, not even knowing how to deposit a check, much less manage accounts. Don't let that happen to you. There are two rules to follow when it comes to managing your finances well: 1) do not accumulate debt and 2) save as much as you can. I learned to master both with time and experience, hitting a few roadblocks along the way.

Pay Your Debts

In the United States, people are drowning in credit card debt. We tend to forget that if we're not careful, that piece of plastic we use for everything can also rob us of the financial independence we've worked so hard to attain. Do not depend on credit cards, and do not let them ruin your financial life. If you are already in debt, take control now.

I was fairly young when I got my first credit cards. (The credit card companies often prey on young, inexperienced people who don't know what they're getting themselves into when they sign up.) Like many young people with new cards, in the blink of an eye, I found myself with debt beyond what I could pay on time. Consequently, I lost my credit for seven years. To pay my bills, I established what I called the "hat raffle": I threw all my bills into a hat, put my hand in and pulled out two. Those were the two I would pay that month, while the rest had to wait until the following month. Slowly but surely, I learned to control my expenses and not waste money. The secret is to understand that making money takes a lot of hard work, but mindless spending is very easy. It's like getting fat: It takes a lot of discipline to slim down, but no effort at all to eat dessert.

If you're already in debt—be it a small or large sum—take the necessary measures to get rid of it. The "hat raffle" is one option; however, it's not a very good one. Most experts will agree that the following five simple steps will help you get back on track:

1. Do not be afraid to ask for help. If your debt is out of control and you don't know what to do, ask for professional help to lower the amount you owe and manage your finances. It's not unlike seeking a nutritionist or a personal trainer to lose weight and get in shape.

2. Make a list of all of your credit cards with outstanding balances, including information such as the account number, due date, total balance, and annual interest. This will help you stay organized and keep track of how much you owe to each company.

3. Stop using credit cards. If you continue to use the credit card you're struggling to pay off, it will become a frustrating, vicious cycle. Some people take the cards out of their wallets and put them away; others cut them up to avoid the temptation of using them. Do whatever is necessary to stop using them. The goal is to get rid of that debt.

4. Pay more than the minimum payment required per month. A credit card's minimum payment mostly goes toward your debt's annual interest. If you pay more than the minimum, you will be able to reduce your debt

more quickly, because whatever you pay above the minimum will go straight to your main balance.

5. Focus on paying the card with the highest annual interest fees first. Once you've finished paying it off, move on to the next card with the highest interest fees (meanwhile, continue paying down the rest of your cards, slightly over the minimum required if possible), and so forth until you are able to say good-bye to your entire debt.

Remember, it's like following a diet: If you watch what you eat and exercise, you'll feel better and lose weight. In this case, if you watch what you spend and take the necessary steps to pay off your debt, you will be on the right path to securing your financial well-being. And, when you're finally financially healthy, as with a diet, once in a while you will be able to splurge on a treat, like that pair of shoes you've been eyeing.

Knowledge Is Power

If you need help managing your finances and paying off your debt, call American Consumer Credit Counseling, a nonprofit organization that offers services such as financial counseling, management, and education: 800-769-3571.

Save

"Save for a rainy day," goes the old adage, and today I understand that better than ever. But I didn't always get it, and it's still hard for me to apply this rule to my own life. The idea of saving doesn't exactly come naturally to me. My first reaction is always:

Save for what? If a truck runs me over, what did I spend my life saving for? There is definitely a time and place to enjoy your earnings, but on a daily basis, this isn't a very responsible way of thinking, especially if you have children who depend on you.

Today, thanks to my husband Marcos and to my own life experiences, I have realized that saving is absolutely essential. My thinking used to be that money was something that can always be attained. I was never short of money-making opportunities. Be it with sixteen jobs at once or just one, I always knew I could make a living doing something. Therefore, for many years I thought, *If the money runs out, you go out and make more.* Now I know that, although this may be true for some people, the importance of saving applies to everyone, whether we put money away for emergencies, our children's education, or retirement.

Many of the arguments Marcos and I have involve money. He grew up in a poor family where he learned to save, and I come from a rich family where I learned that if we lost money, more was just around the corner. Finally, one day Marcos said to me, "And when you get old, with all the ailments you will have, when you can no longer even get out of bed to work, what are you going to do? That's why we have to save." He couldn't have been more right.

During the past ten years, given my son's bipolar diagnosis, my mother's Alzheimer's disease, and my own personal health battles, which I will go into detail in the book, I've never been more grateful for our savings. What would have happened to us without it? We would have likely been drowning in debt, having to spend most of our lives paying it off rather than healing and peacefully enjoying our golden years. I give credit to Marcos for teaching me the importance of saving, and he loves it when I say that. Nonetheless, it's also important to find a balance: We must enjoy the fruits of our labor occasionally while still feeling the security of having savings set aside.

How to Manage Money Within a Couple

One of the biggest challenges a couple faces is finding a financial managing system that works for both people, and this includes one that allows you to maintain your financial independence so you never feel tied to or 100 percent dependent on anyone. This is a very personal decision; some couples manage just fine with one joint account. What matters is that you communicate with your partner and agree on a system that works for the relationship.

Our system was established when Marcos became my representative. I work and earn my own money, but he manages it, as would any artist's representative. Since Marcos is more organized than I am and has a clearer sense of saving and managing finances, he pays the bills and lets me know if I need to curb my spending, so we can stay within our budget. This is what works for us.

One of my producers and her husband, also a TV producer, have been married for several years and still maintain their money in separate accounts. When it's time to pay the bills, they distribute them evenly and share the overall living expenses. For other couples, the woman may be the one managing the finances. Again, it's important to remember that one system won't work for everyone. You must discover which one is best for you and your partner.

Another important factor to keep in mind is that most couples go through different life stages, which in turn may influence how they handle their finances through the years. Maybe at first each person pays his or her own bills, but with time they may realize that one partner is more organized than the other and that person then takes on the role of financial manager. It's up to you and your partner to make these decisions as the years pass. You must learn to be flexible to be able to grow, learn, and evolve individually and as a couple.

Independence Lies Within Your Mind

You must always maintain total independence when it comes to your relationship and your own finances. I can't stress that enough and I think I've established that in this chapter. It's clear that without financial independence there is no freedom; however, true independence cannot be found in the money you make, but rather in your mind.

To achieve financial independence and the freedom and equality most women seek, it is essential that you learn to think for yourself. Keep up to date on everything. The better informed you are, the better off you'll be under any circumstance. When you grab a newspaper, don't just jump to the horoscopes, then read the lifestyle section and be done with it. No. You must read every section in the paper. You have to find out

> *To achieve financial independence and the freedom and equality most women seek, it is essential that you learn to think for yourself.*

what's happening in the world, in local, national, and international politics, and don't even think about skipping over the finance section. Finance has nothing to do with the allowance someone gives you for your expenses. You must learn about finance in order to control your own finances.

Independence does not exist without financial independence, and that's a universal fact, regardless of whether you're a man or a woman. And to achieve that independence you must roll up your sleeves and work very, very hard. Always put your heart and soul into whatever you do, and stay passionate. I hope you find the inspiration to do that in the next chapter. Keep reading, because this is only the beginning.

PUT IT TO WORK FOR YOU!

1. To achieve true independence you must attain financial independence. Never depend on anyone 100 percent.
2. Learn how to make a living not only to become independent, but also to protect your children's well-being if you suddenly find yourself single or widowed.
3. Get rid of your credit card debt and learn how to save for tomorrow (for both your children's education and your golden years).
4. Talk with your partner and choose a financial system that works for the both of you and will put you ahead monetarily.
5. Stay informed and continue learning so you can think for yourself and achieve independence of mind, which is even more valuable than financial freedom.

2

To Succeed in Life You Must Follow Your Heart

Many think that talented people are born with a vocation, but I don't agree. People aren't born with a calling; it's something that slowly develops throughout life. We discover our talents and skills when we nurture our passions and abilities. Some people find their vocations at a young age, while

> *People aren't born with a calling; it's something that slowly develops throughout life.*

others discover it later, and some have to simply go out and actively search for it. This last group of people must nourish that inner seed, so that it may flourish and grow as they discover what makes them happy. It's not an easy journey, but it's an essential one.

I now know that I was born to teach and motivate people; communication comes naturally to me, but I discovered this only with time and experience. As a child, I didn't even watch TV; I wasn't interested in it. I spent my days reading and writing. All I wanted was to be a writer. I loved writing. I always kept a notebook handy to jot down my thoughts, my worries, and my dreams. If I didn't capture them on paper, they didn't feel real.

When I began my university studies and the time came for me to choose a major, my dad asked what career I had in mind, and, without a moment's hesitation, I quickly blurted out, "I want to be a writer."

But my father, having worked in the print business as long as my grandfather, since it was the family business, was less than pleased with my answer. "You're going to starve to death," he said when he heard this. He then broke it down for me and explained that very few writers were able to support themselves with pen and paper. Plus, since we were exiled—having come from Cuba in the early sixties—it was important for me to choose a career that would allow me to make a living, as well as one that would feed my passions. So he suggested an alternative: "You should learn to type so you can be a journalist, and that way you'll get paid regularly."

Since making a living as a journalist was more feasible, I said good-bye to writing and hello to journalism. Through journalism, I found my voice and my vocation: to teach and motivate people. In 1973, I left *Vanidades* and accepted a position as an editor for *Cosmopolitan en Español*. Working for the magazine gave me the chance to write about feminism as the movement unfolded before our eyes, and having the chance to learn about this issue wasn't the only thing that I found fascinating—I loved being able to share it with readers. Teaching and motivating people filled me, and continue to fill me, with satisfaction and happiness.

Knowledge Is Power

Merriam-Webster's Dictionary defines a "calling" as "the vocation or profession in which one customarily engages." And it defines "vocation" as "a summons or strong inclination to a particular state or course of action."

Discover Your Calling

Finding your calling, if you still haven't managed to define what it is, takes a lot of hard work. And simply dreaming about it won't get you closer to discovering it. It takes trial and error and years of experience to find your place in this world. Focus, do the research, ask questions, pay attention, and explore the things that make you happy. If something interests you, try it. You never know what door may open. In that instance, don't worry too much about the future. First you have to focus on looking for something to do that makes you happy. Afterward, you can set goals so that whatever you love to do can become your career—and your livelihood.

Start by asking yourself some basic questions and make sure to be completely honest when you answer them. If you aren't honest with yourself, there's no point in even doing this exercise. You can use the following questions to help you begin to discover the path toward your true calling. Write the answers down on a piece of paper or in a notebook, and reread them later to see if something that you might be curious to explore further jumps out at you.

1. What do you like to do? What are you passionate about? Think about your hobbies and the things you do that make you feel happy and fulfilled.
2. What are you good at? Concentrate on your skills, on what you know you do well. Think about when those around you ask for your help—what is it usually for?
3. If money was no obstacle, what would you choose to do with your life? What would you do just for the pure pleasure of doing it, if you didn't have to worry about whether your survival depended on it? Think about your passion, your purpose in this world, and what brings you the most joy.

It's essential to be honest in answering these questions. This is the first step toward discovering your own career—and your calling. Don't limit yourself by thinking you couldn't possibly earn money doing what you love to do. The object of posing these questions is simply to discover your passion.

Also keep in mind that you might find more than one passion; that's when analyzing your skills can come in handy. If you love doing more than one thing, which of the two can you actually do well? Answering these questions will help you focus on how you can transform what you love to do into a career.

Many times, what we see as impossible is actually possible. We often believe that it's impossible to turn our passion into a career, but that's simply not true. It is most definitely possible. Think about it. Are you a good listener? Do you give good advice? If so, you could consider becoming a counselor or psychologist. Do you love animals? Then think about working at a pet shop or becoming a veterinarian.

You can start small. I have a friend who was studying journalism in college, but music was her passion. When looking for part-time work to help pay for tuition, she got a job at a music store located near the city's most important music college. There, she met many musicians who soon began offering her gigs to sing with different bands throughout the city. That job at the music store not only helped her pay for her education, where she majored in one of her passions, but also led to paid work in music, her other passion in life. Sometimes you might not pay attention to everything at your fingertips. But if you don't keep your eyes open, you risk losing out on great opportunities, so always keep in mind that you may have more than one calling and be ready to follow your heart.

Knowledge Is Power

What Color Is Your Parachute?, by Richard N. Bolles, published in 1970 and revised every year since 1975, is considered the go-to guide for discovering your skills and your passions, so you can find a job doing what you love and what you're good at. It can be another good tool to help find your calling.

I believe that everyone has one or more natural abilities. But for some people, those skills may not match the career path they have chosen. At times that can be quite frustrating. You shouldn't be afraid of change, because with each change in your life, you can discover something new that you're capable of doing.

Start Doing What You Love, Now

If you feel you don't have any clear calling, if you feel the days are passing you by without finding your true passion, it's important to set out to find it. If you stay seated with your arms crossed without investigating various possibilities or asking yourself the necessary questions, you will never find that passion, that calling, that one thing that you love doing, where the hours fly by without you even noticing. To arrive at that place in your life after asking yourself questions and considering where to begin, it's essential to act.

Find a job in an area that interests you. If you dream of becoming a chef, then get a job at a restaurant. That could be the first step toward achieving your big goal. You never know what doors may open, but if you don't go for it, you will always wonder "What if?" One job can lead you to another job or to something else, and slowly but surely your path will become clearer. When you begin to take these steps, don't get discouraged if some doors close or if some of your attempts fail. Every experience is important, and little by little you will begin saying to yourself, not here, not here either, but here, yes! Action and experience are essential for you to begin learning what you're good at and what you're not.

Take, for example, my career in Spanish. Developing a career in Spanish was not in my plans and something that fell into my lap almost by accident. Ever since arriving in the United States at the age of twelve, my entire education had been in English. I learned to become a writer through the English language and certainly didn't have the skills to write in Spanish the way I did in English. So, when I suddenly found myself with a job at *Vanidades*, a magazine that is distributed to twenty-three Spanish-speaking countries, I had no other choice but to teach myself how to write in Spanish. I would sit with an English/Spanish dictionary on my lap and look up any word I didn't know how to say in Spanish.

Was working in Spanish my passion? No. My career in Spanish began like this because it was the job I had at the time and the chance to rise up and shine as a journalist presented itself through this opportunity. And I'm not one to step away from a challenge; I grabbed this job and made it mine.

When opportunities strike, always, always, always take advantage of them. You have to be aware of what comes your way, because if you are unable to see what's right in front of your nose, you may miss out on amazing possibilities. Don't be afraid of trying new things, those you've always been curious about but never imagined yourself doing. But I would advise against doing something you dislike—even if you think it's a good idea—because it will not work; you will not be good at it because your heart won't be in it. And if you're not good at what you do, you will feel frustrated and unhappy, when what you should be searching for is a career that you can be passionate about.

Remember, no matter what you do, follow your heart and give it all you've got. You must be open-minded in life because you never know when and where you'll find a new passion. Ten years ago, when Marcos and I moved to

> *What you should be searching for is a career that you can be passionate about.*

the house we call home today, we were looking for a life change. We needed peace. We used to live in Miami Beach, on an island, and the location turned out to be a source of stress—too many paparazzi, too much craziness. Our home no longer made us happy. That's how we came upon this quieter and more private neighborhood.

The house came with some built-in fishponds in the back-yard made for Japanese fish called koi, and this sparked Marcos's curiosity. This curiosity turned into his new hobby, and this hobby quickly became his new passion. He has now earned great respect within the group of people who own these fish in the area. That's why I can't emphasize enough how important it is to be open to new things, because you never know where your next passion may be hiding. That's what life is all about. You must allow your universe to constantly spread and grow.

Once you've put into action your vocational search, make sure you have the necessary support, be it a family member, a friend, or, better yet, a mentor (see chapter 4, "Find a Mentor, Pay

Knowledge Is Power

There are endless amounts of online resources that share information on different careers. Here's one I found called CareerOneStop, sponsored by the U.S. Department of Labor. Start with the first tab, Explore Careers, to learn more about a variety of careers in several industries. If something catches your eye, look for more information on that specific line of work and take action. You will never know what's at the other side of the door if you don't push it open. www.careeronestop.org/ExploreCareers/ExploreCareers.aspx

Attention, and Learn"). With your curiosity and the support of at least one person, you will be able to continue learning and diving into this new journey in your life. As time goes by, you will realize that following your heart and doing what you love only pushes you to be better at what you do. And that is truly priceless.

The Difference Between a Career and a Job

A job and a career are two very different concepts. Knowing what makes them different is the key to success. A job is something you do till five thirty or six p.m. If all you can think about is the start and end of your workday and you're eager to return to your life outside of work, you are definitely not on a career path. A career encompasses your entire life; it's your passion; it's all you strive to achieve. For a career, you are willing to get to work early, leave late, and do whatever it takes to acquire more knowledge in your field and move ahead without even seeing it as a sacrifice or duty. You do it because you love it.

If you don't feel that passion at work, you're in the wrong place. Let's use one of my employees as an example. He was with me for twenty years, but did not like working. He said that Marcos and I were workaholics who were missing out on life. In the end, that life he so admired slipped through his fingers. He ended up getting a divorce, being fired, and losing the chance to have the life he had supposedly visualized. Instead of focusing on his future, paying attention to what he wanted to achieve, and working toward that goal, he cared only about heading home from work on time.

Aside from having spent years observing people who don't

take their careers seriously, I also know what it's like to feel stuck at a job. In 1976, I decided to make another career move. I left my position at *Cosmopolitan en Español* for a better-paid one at the *Miami Herald*, a newspaper that at the time was experiencing rapid-fire growth. However, after six months on the job, I was bored. My career as a journalist had started on an international platform both at *Vanidades* and *Cosmopolitan en Español*, so I felt that the walls were slowly closing in on me at the *Miami Herald*. My career was becoming just a job, and that was completely unacceptable to me.

Given these circumstances, I decided to turn my focus on another dream I hoped to make a reality: starting a family. I got married, had my daughter Titi, and left my job in order to dedicate myself to my family. However, after a while, money became tight, so Tony—Titi's father and my ex-husband—asked if I would consider going back to work. I quickly reminded him that I had put my career on hold to start a family with him; if I went back to work, he had to understand that to me that meant picking up where I had left off with my career. I'm not the type to simply go to a nine-to-five job and return home without yearning for more; that's what having a job is, and I have always strived to continue developing my career, which is exactly what I ended up doing.

You know what your God-given gifts are—I'm talking about the things you are great at, the skills that bring you happiness and satisfaction. Follow that path and give yourself the chance to have a career you are passionate about instead of a simple and tedious job. A good example of what can come from not being afraid to trade a job for a career you are passionate about is my makeup artist's story. Miguel Ángel Pérez used to work at a bank. You have no idea how much he hated that job. It made him so unhappy. He eventually reached his limits and decided to follow his passion, his calling: He became a professional makeup artist. Today, he is one of the best makeup artists in the industry. If he hadn't taken that leap of faith to follow his passion, he'd probably still be frustrated and unhappy at a job that only amounted to a paycheck.

SHARING THE TRUTH

If you are constantly watching the clock at work, it's time to reevaluate your career choices and make a change. You must seek out inspiration in what you do. If you work for only the money, you will be miserable. It's clear we all need money to survive, but money alone will not bring you happiness. If you don't do what you love in life, no matter how much money you make, you will never be truly happy. Follow your heart.

My career makes me happy. If you find that happiness, that passion for your career, you will see that it will push you to become a better person overall. Communication is my calling. I'm a communicator; it doesn't matter how I do it, that's what moves me to the core and fills me with joy. I love motivating people, and Marcos made me realize I had this skill many years ago, when I was the editor in chief at *Cosmopolitan en Español*. As editor in chief, I strove to go beyond talking about women's sexual liberation. I wanted to turn the magazine into a guide that motivated Latina women to aspire to higher goals and improve all facets of their lives.

Around that time, Marcos and I stopped by a department store's makeup aisle. At the time, I did not yet have my TV show, and while I was paying for my stuff, the woman at the counter looked up and said, "Cristina Saralegui, I want you to know that you changed my life." "How?" I asked. And she replied, "I got a divorce because you left Tony." This woman had read my magazine column where I described the end of my marriage with my first husband, and my story inspired her and helped her make a huge life decision: She left her abusive husband and came to the United States with her children. As we walked away, Marcos said, "Hey, do you realize how inspiring you are to people?"

No, I hadn't realized it. But I'm not just the motivator; I'm also the one being motivated. People are my inspiration. Do you know who I enjoy interviewing the most? Regular, everyday people who are absolutely amazing. I've interviewed celebrities for years, and most usually have their guard up. They like to show only one side of their personalities, one dimension, to maintain their perfect images. The audience learns nothing from that. People learn from their mistakes, and celebrities don't like to talk about what they've done wrong; they just want to promote their new CD or new book while of course maintaining the illusion that they are perfect.

> *Find a career that will feed your passions and challenge you to grow.*

I'd rather dedicate my time to discovering ordinary people with extraordinary stories and lessons. Recently, I interviewed a brilliant American immigration lawyer who spoke perfect

Spanish. The stories that young man shared with me left me in awe. When I asked him where he had learned Spanish, he answered, "A little in Barcelona, another bit in Mexico, and some from the Cubans and Puerto Ricans in Miami." Everything he said on the radio show was sharp. I loved his intelligence and the ways he found solutions to what seemed like impossible situations. He is practical and dynamic, the type of person you want on your team. And it's funny how looks can be deceiving, because, at first sight, I probably wouldn't have thought about asking him to be on my show. He is blond and all-American, and it wouldn't have dawned on me that he could speak even a lick of Spanish. Also, he came to the studio wearing his running gear, sneakers and all. But his confidence surpassed all expectations and appearances. I love it when people surprise me.

Connecting with people is what I love about my career, and I'm constantly fascinated with the new people I meet and the new things I learn. Instead of settling for a job that just pays the bills, make the necessary changes in your life to find a career that will feed your passions and challenge you to grow and become a better person.

You Can Have More Than One Vocation in Your Life

Vocations develop with time and experience, and can even change along your life journey. Stay focused and work hard to nurture your passions and be open to different opportunities.

For example, Marcos is a much better writer than I am. If he had become a writer instead of a musician, he might have had an amazing writing career because it comes so naturally to him.

But his passion was music and he followed that dream even though it didn't come as easily to him as writing. Yet, through dedication and hard work, he became a good musician. And when his goals and wishes evolved, he did not let fear stop him from changing paths.

When I fell in love with Marcos the musician, I had no idea he would be such a fantastic businessman. Back then, he spent hours practicing, and when Gloria Estefan and the Miami Sound Machine blew up with their mega hit, "Conga," they began touring the world with Marcos as their bass player. With time, Marcos, who was divorced, realized he did not want to jeopardize another marriage with so much traveling and temptation. He wanted to focus and be more present with his family. Although he had been passionate about music his entire life, he was now ready to make his family a priority. His goals had changed, and this shift brought about a career and vocational change in his life and mine. His work no longer fit the life he desired, so he decided to leave the band when they were at the height of success and start again from scratch.

Career and life changes can reveal new skills and open doors to unimaginable places.

Change in general is hard, but it's worth the effort. Leaving the band was an extremely difficult move for Marcos. It was like a sudden free fall until he was able to get his bearings and take off again with his newfound calling in the business world. Marcos became so good at what he did that there was a time when we didn't even need lawyers for our contracts because he took care of it all. If he hadn't taken a leap of faith and changed his career path halfway through the journey, he may have never discovered this amazing hidden talent. Career and life changes can reveal new skills and open doors to unimaginable places.

Marcos is the perfect example of how having more than one vocation in life is absolutely possible. The success we've had together is living proof! Don't tie yourself down to just one path; don't be afraid of change. You may have one lifelong vocation or two or three; remain open-minded. If you find yourself heading down a different road and developing new interests and passions, don't be afraid to explore them. The key is to do what you love, something that has a purpose and makes you happy. Even if it entails doing more than one thing!

Your Children's Callings

Don't follow your parents' dreams, follow your own. And if you don't have any dreams, find them. By the same token, don't ever impose your own dreams on your children. They must discover their own passions and vocations, whatever makes *them* happy. Marcos and I did not force our children to find a certain career or follow in our footsteps. On the contrary, we urged them to find their own callings. Along the way, we constantly reassured them and let them know that we would support them and celebrate their achievements no matter what careers they chose, and that's exactly what we did.

If you have children, help them discover what they are passionate about and support them in this journey. Encourage them to further explore things they enjoy doing. You never know where a vocation may spring from. If they like to dance, sign them up for dance classes. If they're into sports, encourage them to join their school sports teams. If they want to learn how to play an instrument, find a music tutor or enroll them in a music class. And always, always, always encourage them to read. Keep in mind that a vocation can also be discovered through reading and learning. It's important for your children to have parental support while they develop and discover their own identities and what they're most passionate about.

Passion Helps You Reach Higher Grounds

Passion motivates you, and with motivation you can make your dreams come true. Don't be afraid of the challenge. Fear can stop you from achieving your goals; it can paralyze you. Don't accept fear into your life. Many people don't believe in themselves, but you must believe that you can accomplish whatever you set out to do. Along with motivation, you also need discipline. Don't give up, fight for what you want. When you are passionate about something, you will grow and accomplish more with that passion because it has no limits or boundaries and makes you hungry for more.

> *Passion motivates you, and with motivation you can make your dreams come true.*

Everything we do must be done with zeal and passion. To win in life, you must follow your heart. It's the only way to achieve true success.

PUT IT TO WORK FOR YOU!

1. Define your calling.
2. Spring into action and look for a job in a field that interests you.
3. Take advantage of the opportunities that arise.
4. Replace your job with a career.
5. Don't be afraid of change; your passion will motivate you to reach your dreams.

Goals Will Help Make Your Dreams a Reality

Imagine that you are on a ship at sea with a navigation system and you want to go to Hawaii. What do you put in that GPS? The logical answer is "Hawaii." But what if, instead of "Hawaii," you put in "Istanbul." What will happen? Clearly, you won't arrive in Hawaii! That is a goal, the destination that you put in your GPS in order to arrive at a desired location. The GPS is equivalent to the map of your dreams in life, where you write down your goals and the paths you've tried to take to complete them. With this map in hand, you can turn your dreams into reality. Think about it: If you don't know where you're going, you're going to be a little bit lost in life, without knowing in which direction to steer because you don't know what really makes you happy. And if you don't know where you're headed, you will never get anywhere.

We all want to succeed professionally, in love, in family relationships, but to do that we must ask ourselves various questions, beginning with how we define success for ourselves. To find your purpose, ask yourself what do you want? What's important to you? What do you want to accomplish within the different areas of your life? For me, it was important to achieve certain goals that would help me build the life that I wanted: to stand up for myself, to make enough money that I could avoid depending on anyone, to not be invisible, and to give a voice to those who are not heard.

Open your eyes and look around to discover what inspires you, what catches your attention, what you desire. Visualize yourself in the future, how you'd like to live, what you'd love to accomplish in your life. Marcos, for example, came from a poor family. While growing up, he knew only his neighborhood and what surrounded him. When he began to play with Gloria and Emilio Estefan's band the Miami Sound Machine, new doors opened for him. They played private parties at the Gables Estate and inside enormous houses in Miami Beach. Suddenly, he thought, *Hold on, this actually exists? This is what I want. I want to have a waterfront house one day.* And years later, that dream became a reality.

When you establish what your goals are, create a plan to achieve them and follow through with that plan. But stay flexible. You might encounter unexpected twists and turns in life, and like with a GPS, you might have to find another way to get to your destination. Be mindful of alternate routes and be prepared to make some changes to your plan of action in case you encounter a few bumps along the road. Many times, when you achieve a goal or a dream, if you look back, you will notice that you

> *If you stay focused, nothing will stop you from reaching your final destination.*

didn't necessarily reach it by taking the planned route from the point at which your journey first began. But, if you stay focused, nothing will stop you from reaching your final destination.

Set Short- and Long-Term Goals

Earlier, we compared your map of goals with a GPS. Now let's visualize it differently. This map can also be seen as a building's blueprint, and you are the architect. First, as any architect will do, you must draw the blueprint. In your case, drawing your blueprint means taking a moment to think about your dreams and how you plan to make them come true; you must set your short- and long-term goals. The blueprint is only the beginning, but it is an essential step in the entire process. And once the blueprints are drawn, the hard work begins; it is time to begin construction.

In other words, the purpose of setting goals is to help you stay focused on the bigger picture. But simply following the blueprint is not enough. You must be ready to roll up your sleeves and get to work.

Long-term goals do not happen overnight (just like the construction of a building). Don't despair. Be patient, keep sowing those seeds and watering them, and soon you'll reap the fruits of your labor. Meanwhile, create short-term goals to accomplish your long-term goals, because you can accomplish those in less time. For example, your goal may be to take a photography class because you enjoy taking pictures. By going to school, signing up and beginning to take classes, you will complete one of your short-term goals. The purpose of the class may be simply to

> *One goal can lead to another, and another, and another. It's up to you to decide what road you want to take to get there.*

learn more about photography and develop this hobby; however, there is also the chance that this short-term goal will open a door to a new goal, such as becoming a professional photographer. If this is the case, you will have to come up with a series of short-term goals to reach this more long-term goal. As you can see, one goal can lead to another, and another, and another. It's up to you to decide what road you want to take to get there.

I set my first goals when I was twelve years old, while we were living in Key Biscayne. My sister and I were helping set the table when I asked my mom, "So why doesn't my brother have to set the table?" I'd noticed how only the women took on this task, and I didn't understand why the men didn't do it too. So my mom answered with one of her tidbits of wisdom, "Because in life everyone must justify their existence through work. Men work outside and bring the money home. Women support them by working at home. We wash the dishes, cook, and take care of all the household chores." I hated house chores, such as washing dishes, cooking, and setting the table, so in that instant I realized that I would have to work hard outside of the house to make money and bring it home to my family. And that's how I set my first long-term goal: Work hard and avoid the kitchen at all costs.

Let's go back to the building example. To achieve a long-term goal, you must set specific short-term goals to help you accomplish your dream. In this case, to have a livable building, you must start with the basics, the foundation. Then the walls must go up. You'll also need electricity and plumbing work done, as well as several coats of paint. Each one of these steps is a goal that must be reached to finally achieve the long-term one: the finished building. Without these previous steps, there will be no building.

Another great perk that comes with short-term goals is that when you reach them you'll be able to actually feel you are moving toward the bigger goals. Your progress becomes tangible. It's like seeing the light at the end of the tunnel become brighter as you approach it. The satisfaction that comes with accomplishing your goals, both the short- and long-term ones, is invaluable. Always remember that if you divide your big dreams into short-term goals, it is more likely that you will make them come true.

> *If you divide your big dreams into short-term goals, it is more likely that you will make them come true.*

To set these goals, you must continue asking yourself some key questions that will help you discover the road ahead of you. Write down all of your answers and reread them to see what jumps out as something important that you want to accomplish in your life. That's a goal. While doing this exercise, you must be very specific. For example, if you say, "I want to be rich," well, what does being rich mean to you? How much money do you need to make in order to be what you consider rich? Does being rich simply refer to the dollar value, or does it include other aspects of your life?

You must reach deep into your heart, mind, and soul to find

honest answers. That's why I always say that ambition comes in different sizes and that goals must be adapted to what you want. In my case, I have no interest in being as famous as Michael Jackson or Madonna. Fame is a double-edged sword. There's a moment when you reach a limit, and we all have our own set of limits that we do not want to cross. I like having money so that I don't have to worry about it, but I wouldn't want money to be the only thing that motivates me in life, and I know plenty of people like this. When setting your goals, don't just work for the money; if you do something that you love, and you're good at it, money will come along on its own. Focus instead on building the road toward happiness.

SHARING THE TRUTH

You can set goals for every aspect of your life: professional, personal, and spiritual. However, there is one area that many overlook: health. This is usually not considered something you'd set goals for, but listen up: Life is useless without your health. You can set all the goals you want and map them out down to the very last detail of what you want to get out of life, but if you forget to include your health, that map is useless. Health is an essential goal that we must all have on our lists, because without it, we cannot accomplish the rest.

Visible Goals Are Doable Goals

Once you have asked yourself all of the basic questions necessary for you to recognize which goals are the most important in each area of your life, it's time to write them down. When you commit them to paper, type them into your computer, or pin them on your bulletin board, it will be easier for you to visualize and accomplish them. You can use whatever method works. With time, this method may change, but what's important is that your goals remain visible.

When someone wants to lose weight, many experts recommend that the person grab a photo of when she or he was thinner, or of someone with a body that person admires, and put it up on the fridge as a daily reminder and motivator. Writing down your goals serves the same purpose. Find a special notebook or open a new document on your computer and use it only for your goals. Pick whatever method you prefer, but please write them down somewhere. Thinking about your goals is not enough. If you don't write them down, you could forget some of them or they could lose importance. The secret is to think visibly. When you write things down, they materialize. This helps you accomplish what you want, and also helps you evaluate what you still have to achieve.

When writing down your goals, it is extremely important to be very specific. If you want to have a big house, ask yourself how big and where you want it to be located. A big house could mean something entirely different to you than it does to someone else. It's also essential that your goals have end dates. Set daily, weekly, monthly, annual, and long-term goals, and write down the dates by which you'd like to accomplish each one. This will help you stay on the right track. To establish the date, always ask yourself, *When?* When do you want to own that house? When do you want to have your own business? Setting deadlines forces you to be accountable and allows you to see if you're achieving what you've set out to do within the desired time frame, if you're giving yourself enough time, or if maybe you aren't doing all it takes to reach your goal.

Being this specific will lead you to something called "visualization." We will talk more in depth about this in chapter 19, "Spirituality Is Grounding," but for now it's key to make the connection between the importance of setting clear goals and achieving them. Visualizing those goals, picturing them in such detail, has helped me reach all of my accomplishments.

Knowledge Is Power

Merriam-Webster's Dictionary defines the word "visualize" as follows: "to form a visual mental image of something not present before the eye at the time."

I began visualizing what I wanted during my first marriage, at a time when visualization wasn't as popular as it is today; it wasn't in style. I simply did it by instinct. It also was related to my job at the time. Since I ran a magazine, I had to stay up to date with what other magazines were publishing, just as book publishers must read other companies' best sellers to stay on top of their game. Well, while reading these other magazines, I cut out articles and images that I found inspiring for our own. I read magazines from other parts of the world—France, Italy—and doing so was like traveling around the world. Through these articles, I discovered that life truly has a lot of great things to offer, and that's how I began to cut out images of what I hoped to accomplish in my life. Looking back, I now realize that this was my first real venture into what is now known as visualization. Visualization then became an essential tool to achieve my goals and dreams, both in the short and long term.

The Secret to Accomplishing Your Goals

Achieving your goals is not easy—it isn't easy for anyone—but if you focus and work hard, you will make it happen. It's the power of visualization and the law of attraction combined. Your worst enemy on this road is negativity. Steer clear of anything that holds you back, anchors you down in one place, and doesn't let you rise up and shine. You don't want any detractors in your life. Surround yourself with positive and caring people—those who support you and encourage you to keep working toward achieving your goals and accomplishing your dreams even when you think you can't. Those are the people and the energy that will help you reach your goals and live your dreams.

If others have been able to reach their goals and dreams, so can you. Find out how the people you admire became successful. Pay attention to the discipline and hard work they put into their journeys to reach their desired destinations. Learn from them and use their stories to inspire you to set your own goals and achieve whatever you want in life (see chapter 4, "Find a Mentor, Pay Attention, and Learn"). If you work hard and have a positive outlook, anything is possible.

Everything you do should be done with a zest for life. Otherwise we risk living our lives like robots without passion,

Knowledge Is Power

According to a study by WomanWise, women are redefining what achieving the American Dream means to them, and it doesn't include the white picket fence. Visions of the classic suburban home, 2.5 kids, and financial independence supported by a successful husband have become a thing of the past as women today become more self-reliant and independent.

dreams, or goals. Some people are simply not persistent enough; if something doesn't go their way from the get-go, they immediately give up. Don't let the wave break into your life and wash away your dreams. Nothing will happen to you if you don't go out and search, create, and fight for what you want.

So, to accomplish both your short- and long-term goals, you must add these five principles to your life:

1. Passion
2. Motivation
3. Self-Discipline
4. Perseverance
5. Flexibility

1. Passion

We've spoken at length about how important it is to be passionate about what you do, but it's worth mentioning once again. Never try to dedicate yourself to something you don't enjoy doing, because that will become simply a job instead of a career. To succeed in life, you must follow your heart and do what you love. Without passion, you will not find the necessary motivation to achieve your goals.

2. Motivation

There is negative motivation and positive motivation. Many people spend their time watching what everyone else is doing and comparing themselves to others to achieve the same thing. That's negative motivation. Why? Well, because you lose a lot of time focusing on what the rest of the world is doing instead of concentrating on your own life. If you continue down this road, you will never be happy because the person next to you will always have something that you don't. You must live your own life and be happy with what you do and what *you* accomplish.

When you focus on your own journey and notice how certain plans or goals become a reality, you become filled with positive motivation that continually propels you forward until you make your dreams come true. Take Marcos, for example. His goal was to become a musician, to become famous, to travel the world, and to earn money. And, with a lot of time and effort, he made it happen. Find the source of inspiration that will fill you with the motivation you need to keep pushing forward. The journey is far from easy, but if you keep your passion and motivation alive, you'll see that the effort is well worth it.

> *The journey is far from easy, but if you keep your passion and motivation alive, you'll see that the effort is well worth it.*

3. Self-Discipline

Big goals take longer to accomplish. They are the dreams that we hope to transform into a reality, that destination we long to reach with all our hearts. To arrive at that destination, one of the basic tools you need is self-discipline. You must get up day after day and stay focused on what you want to accomplish. It's like with everything in life—discipline is essential to achieve what we set out to do.

Some people have talent, but are lost because they don't apply themselves due to lack of self-discipline. Others have clear goals but also lack the self-discipline to achieve them. We all need discipline. Whether you're feeling inspired or not, you must have the discipline to work regardless and, by doing so, it's possible that the inspiration you were looking for will appear before your eyes. Everything is connected, so use it in your favor.

Discipline goes hand in hand with organization and time management. Today, there are way too many distractions, such as Facebook, Twitter, e-mail, your cell phone, kitten videos on the Internet, and all of that just eats up your precious time—time you could be using to reach your goals. I'm not saying you have to stop using social media and the Internet, simply that you have to learn how to manage your time so that these distractions do not occupy valuable hours of your day. Get organized. Take a look at how you use the hours in your day and find the time needed to make the efforts your goals require, be it learning something new, sending résumés to companies that interest you, spending more moments with your family, or sharing your time with those in need.

4. Perseverance

Sometimes when you begin learning and studying something difficult, you might not get it at first and you inevitably feel stuck. So you read it and study it again, but you still don't quite get it. And maybe by the tenth time you go over it, the concept clicks and you finally fully grasp it and make it yours. That's called perseverance. When I moved into the TV world, I was awful at reading the teleprompter. However, instead of letting that frustration paralyze me, I did something about it. I practiced and took lessons on how to read in a way that sounded natural. Never give up—persevere and constantly improve your skills.

You can accomplish whatever you set your mind to if you focus and don't give up. Don't be afraid. Every problem has a solution. And get ready, you will encounter a lot of bumps in the road, many unexpected turns, but you can't let these roadblocks prevent you from reaching your destination. Instead of giving up when encountering something you are unsure of, face your doubts and fears head-on and say the following out loud: "I'm capable of learning this. I'm capable of doing this." Because you are! You just have to believe in yourself and persevere. Keep trying. If one path doesn't work, find an alternate road. You will see that perseverance will bring amazing results.

> *You can accomplish whatever you set your mind to if you focus and don't give up.*

5. Flexibility

Flexibility is last on this list of secrets to help you reach your goals, but it's just as important as the rest. If you're passionate about what you do, are motivated, and have self-discipline and perseverance, but aren't flexible, you will likely hit a wall at some point in your journey. Because if you're going down a road and stumble upon a roadblock, and you believe that's the only road that can possibly take you to your destination, you'll be stuck there without being able to move forward. However, if you are flexible in mind and spirit, if you set your rigidity aside, you can probably look around and find an alternate path that will take you around the corner of that wall so that you can continue moving forward toward your dream.

When you set your goals, you must be open to change and willing to explore different paths to reach them. You never know what obstacles you might run into, but if you're flexible, you'll be able to work through life's unexpected twists and turns toward your dream destination without losing your way. Remember: Perfectionism is the enemy of success.

> *Perfectionism is the enemy of success.*

When you try something and it doesn't work out, and you just keep repeating the same actions because you're trying to perfect them again and again, you can die from trying because you lack flexibility. You must be willing to travel down a different road if you see that the one you're on is littered with too many obstacles. There are always other alternatives; however, if you are a perfectionist and inflexible, you will never give yourself the opportunity to see other avenues that might take you to the same place. Doing the same thing over and over again and expecting different results is the definition of insanity. That's not me, and I hope that's not you, either. You have to try everything and find alternate routes. Your cleverness and creativity could surprise you.

Adjust Your Goals to Your Life Changes

As you grow and learn, your goals will tend to change, especially during life-defining moments, such as when you head off to college, when you leave one job for another, or when you start a family. When you reach these milestones, you must stop and give yourself time to think and reflect. Review your personal map, evaluate and adjust your goals, and choose the next path to success and happiness.

My main goal when I began college was to be a writer, but I decided to follow my father's advice and major in journalism. When I did that, my main goal was crystal clear: I would make my living as a journalist, but I would eventually dedicate myself to writing. However, with time and added responsibilities, I realized I had to take care of my parents, my family at home, and my work family, and the goal of becoming a writer was replaced with developing my career as a communicator. With these responsibilities in mind, along with my career, I was motivated to take on better-paying jobs and rise in the ranks, becoming editor in chief at *Cosmopolitan en Español* and then expanding to TV. I remained flexible and open to the new opportunities that life threw my way, and adjusted my goals accordingly.

You shouldn't only rethink your goals with big life changes. You should find whatever method works for you. No matter how you do it, make sure you return to your list of goals, review it and adjust it as necessary to continue moving ahead. When you reread what you've written, you may notice some things have changed in your life, and these changes must be reflected in your goals. You may have already reached certain goals, some dreams may have evolved, and other things may not carry the same importance as before. That's why you should follow these three steps each time you review your goals:

1. When you reach one of your goals, cross it off your list.
2. If you notice outdated goals, remove them from your list or adjust them so they reflect your here and now.
3. Add any new goals that may have appeared in your life.

Reviewing your goals is a basic step for staying up to date with what you want to accomplish in life and what you have already achieved. When you cross a goal off your list, take a moment to remember the path you traveled in order to accomplish it, and congratulate yourself. Let your achievements inspire and motivate you to continue onward. How often you review your list of goals is entirely up to you. You can do so every day, every week, every month—whatever fits your personality and lifestyle.

Some people like to review their goals and add new ones to their list at the start of the New Year. I have a friend who looks over his list of goals on his birthday to see what he has accomplished, what he must change, and what he still has to achieve. I like to review my goals when I experience life changes. I actually recommend that you keep this in mind: Even if you choose another time to review your goals, make sure to always give them a look when you experience a big life-changing moment, be it losing a job, giving birth, experiencing the loss of a loved one, getting married or divorced, or reaching the third stage of your life. These are all key moments that are in need of special attention.

As I've mentioned before, as a young man, Marcos's greatest motivation was to become a musician, be famous, travel, see the world, and make money . . . and he did it. However, along the way, he decided to modify these goals because once he reached a certain stage of his life, he realized that some of his old goals no longer fit his new wants and needs. His desire for fame, travel, and living off of music had changed. Now he wanted to be closer to his family, wake up knowing what city he was in, and have the chance to settle down in one place. So, he changed his goals. Change is not easy, but Marcos learned how to be happy with what he had, and that happiness opened other doors toward new goals and new dreams.

> *Life will let you know when it's time to make new goals.*

Life will let you know when it's time to make new goals. In my case, after twenty-one years at the same company, I lost my job, and suddenly I had to make new goals to continue moving forward. No matter what time of year it is, if you feel the need to review and adjust your goals, do it! Go over them, write them all down, and, most importantly, follow each goal with action. That's what I do. I have an action plan for each one of my goals, and I place my list of goals in a visible place so I can read them every day. I have a bulletin board in my bathroom where I pin my lists and clippings of goals I want to accomplish. I've even left a few things that I have already achieved because it's a daily reminder of the fantastic life I have—sometimes we tend to forget about all the good things that we already have.

So, what will you do once you've reached your goals? Develop more goals! Don't be afraid to dream big and grow. When I married Marcos, I asked him, "What do you expect of me? What do you want?" I didn't want to screw this up like I did with Tony. I wanted everything out in the open. And he answered, "Well, I see us together toward the end of my life with a large table surrounded by children and grandchildren." Instantly, that became one of my goals. And just the other day, during Thanksgiving dinner, I told him, "Open your eyes and look around you, because that's what you have here." Sometimes your goals have already been reached, and you don't even realize it. That's why it's incredibly important to review your list and acknowledge and congratulate yourself when you have done it.

At the end of my autobiography, *Cristina!: My Life as a Blonde*, I described how I saw myself in the future, and I listed some general goals:

> In a not-too-distant future, I see myself in Villa Serena, my home in Miami Beach, with my three children and my grandchildren, writing my books. I see my Marc happy, as he is today, with his successful company, and fulfilling himself more and more as he is able to become involved in those things that truly interest him. I see myself remembering the madness of being the host of a daily television program—

although I believe it has been a most amusing madness, strongly positive. And I see myself giving thanks to God for how happy I have been.

Today, seventeen years later, after rereading this paragraph, I'm deeply moved as I realize that I have achieved those goals. We no longer live in that house (a goal and wish that clearly changed with time), but I am surrounded by my children and grandchildren. Marcos is successful and personally fulfilled in all his interests. And, aside from all the things I do to continue developing my career, I've given myself the time and space to put these thoughts on paper and write this book, where I have used, among other tools, the experiences I gathered throughout the years as a television host to continue motivating anyone and everyone willing to listen. And, in the meantime, I thank God for how happy I am with having been able to make my biggest dreams come true.

Achieving your important goals and making your dreams a reality is not easy, but it is possible. Each goal has a different price. Some will require more sacrifices than others. You may not be able to watch your favorite TV show or attend every one of your children's school events because you will have to dedicate more time to your career. However, if you're willing to make the effort to reach your goals, spending extra time on work will result in a career that will make you proud, and that career for which you had to sacrifice some time will allow you to send your children off to college. If the price and sacrifice your goals require are worth it at the end of the road, *Forward and onward, don't ever look back, not even to gain momentum.*

PUT IT TO WORK FOR YOU!

1. Ask yourself the right questions to set your short- and long-term goals.
2. Create a list of your goals and use the power of visualization to bring forth what you desire.
3. Do what you love, use that passion as a source of motivation, and move forward with self-discipline, perseverance, and flexibility to make your dreams a reality.
4. Review your goals and adjust them according to your life changes.
5. When you've reached your goals, congratulate yourself, and then set more goals, and always follow through with an action plan.

4

Find a Mentor, Pay Attention,
and Learn

We've covered the importance of financial independence, being passionate about what you do, and how to set goals to accomplish your dreams. Once you've taken these initial steps in your life toward the destination you've always dreamed about, the next step is to gain experience through working and learning. You must be a sponge, absorbing all the knowledge you possibly can in life. We should never stop learning. Regardless of age, never let your curiosity dwindle. Keep on learning till your very last day on this Earth.

When you start taking those first steps toward reaching your goals, the level of success you'll achieve will depend on you being open to learning, and the best way to facilitate learning in your career and in your life is to find a mentor.

A mentor will guide, advise, support, and encourage you, as well as keep you focused and on track. She or he is the person you admire and respect, the living example of what you hope to become or accomplish in your life. It could be your mother, your father, an uncle, a cousin, a friend, a colleague, a boss. If some-

Knowledge Is Power

Merriam-Webster's Dictionary's definition of "mentor" is simple and straightforward: "a trusted counselor or guide." The word comes from Greek mythology. Mentor was a friend of Odysseus entrusted with the education of Odysseus's son, Telemachus, and with his palace when he set off for the Trojan War. Athena (the goddess of wisdom, courage, inspiration, and more) disguised herself as Mentor and encouraged Telemachus to search for his father, Odysseus, serving as his counselor. And that is how the meaning of the word "mentor" came to be in our language.

one you admire takes you under his or her wing, take full advantage of this amazing opportunity. Open up and learn from the experience and wisdom of others. Listen, read, pay attention, and ask a lot of questions. If you don't know how to do something, ask your mentor for guidance. You learn by asking questions. If you don't allow yourself to learn and grow because you

> *If you don't know how to do something, the worst mistake you can make is to not ask and learn.*

are too afraid to admit that you don't know how to do something, you'll remain stagnant. You'll never get that promotion you've been eyeing nor will you have the confidence to find bigger and better positions because you were paralyzed by fear. Don't let this be you.

People fear what they don't understand. Learn to control and overcome your fears by taking action. If you don't know how to do something, the worst mistake you can make is to not ask and learn. If you realize you can't do it alone, ask someone for help. Approach the right person and say, "I don't know how to do this. Could you show me?" Ultimately, it's in everyone's best interest. More likely than not, if you ask, you shall receive.

Life Examples

As we go through different stages of life, we hope to surround ourselves with people who inspire us to dream big. They aren't necessarily mentors, but if they inspire you to improve your quality of life, advance your career, share your love with your family and those who most need it, we could call them indirect mentors. You can learn so much if you observe them and understand what made them successful. These people can be an infinite source of motivation. In my life, that person was my grandfather.

My grandfather, Francisco Saralegui, was the third child in a very poor family from the Basque Country. His mom died at childbirth when he was born and his father did not know how to raise children, so my grandfather was handed over to another Basque woman, who had children of her own, and she breast-fed and raised him. In Basque tradition, the eldest son inherits everything; the second one must become a priest; and the third must travel to the Americas to bring back money for the family left behind in the Pyrenees Mountains. My grandfather was the third one; therefore, at twelve, he set sail to the Americas and landed in Argentina. He chose this destination because he had been told his father was there, even though he barely spoke Spanish, only Basque. He tirelessly searched for him to no avail.

Meanwhile, he met another Basque man and ended up staying with him for six years, learning Spanish and working.

He never stopped searching for his father and at long last discovered he had moved to Cuba. So, at seventeen, he grabbed his savings and bought himself a ticket to Cuba. He asked around and found out his father was working as a manager at a sugar factory in Santiago de Cuba. When they finally met after so many years, instead of offering to pay for his education (at this point, he had money to spare), his father put him to work loading sacks of sugar at the docks. Suddenly, it dawned on my grandfather that this wasn't the life he wanted. He grabbed his things and moved to Havana, where he found a job as an elevator operator in an office building. He took night classes and eventually became a bookkeeper. At his elevator job, he heard all the details about the lives of everyone coming and going in that building. He also forged friendships, and one day one of his friends confessed he had money problems. My grandfather, who was a big saver, lent him the money and asked for a modest commission. That same friend later employed him as a bookkeeper at night, after his elevator shift was over. And when this friend once again ran into money troubles due to gambling debts, this time, instead of lending him money, my grandfather bought part of his company shares, and so he went from being an elevator operator to bookkeeper to company shareholder. With time, he would become a major shareholder of that same company, which represented Cuba's interests in foreign companies dealing with insurance, hardware tools, and other businesses. But the most important one was a Canadian company that supplied the island with paper for all its newspapers and magazines. That's where his nickname "The Paper Czar" came from.

Later, he jumped at the opportunity and became co-owner of three of the most important magazines in Latin America: *Bohemia*, *Carteles*, and *Vanidades*. When he died, aside from all his personal and professional accomplishments, he spoke five languages, which he had taught himself. So, with a grandfather like that, admired and adored by everyone in the family, I decided I wanted to be just like him. I needed someone to measure myself against while I sought my own accomplishments and success, and that someone was my grandfather.

If you have someone in your life who inspires you, like my grandfather inspired me, research that person's life and pay attention to how she or he accomplished her or his goals. They are life examples to be followed and important reference points to guide you along your journey to success.

How to Discover Your Mentor

If you're not open to learning from your experiences, from the new things in life that touch you, from the people around you, maybe you're not ready for a mentor. If this is you, I'm asking you right now to find that person or people you admire, begin to notice what they do, what they say, how they advise you, and how that applies to your own life. You don't know how incredible it is to have a mentor; it's another great secret to success at all levels.

Mentors can come from many places. A mentor is a person you admire and respect. As I've mentioned earlier, this person could be a boss, a colleague, a friend, a family member, or someone who simply did something that you find inspiring and want to learn more about. You can have one or more mentors, and you can have different mentors for different areas or moments of your life. Mentors can change as your goals and dreams evolve throughout the different stages of your life. You may already have a mentor and not even know it. If you turn to someone specific for advice because you admire this person and he or she inspires you to be better at what you do, bingo! That person is your mentor!

I was fortunate enough to count on several mentors in my life, but the most important ones have been some of my bosses and friends. The following are a few anecdotes of my beloved mentors. I hope these stories will serve as examples of what you should look for when seeking out your own go-to person and show the infinite rewards of having trusted and wise people in your life.

Elvira Mendoza

My first boss at *Vanidades* was a Colombian woman named Elvira Mendoza—I consider her to be my first journalism teacher. That woman taught me so much. Whenever she assigned a project that I wasn't sure how to do, instead of giving it a shot, the first thing I would do is tell her I didn't know how to do it.

"And how do you know that you don't know?" she would ask me.

"Because I've never done it before," I'd answer.

"Then you don't know if you know. Go and do it. And if

you realize you really can't, then come back and I'll help you," she'd reply.

That's how I learned that first you must try to do what is asked of you. If you try and realize you don't have enough skills to finish the job, don't be afraid to ask for help.

The things I learned from this amazing woman are priceless. Another great lesson I learned from her is that you mustn't rest on your laurels. Because of her, I began my career in Spanish. When I first started working at *Vanidades*, I wrote my articles in English and she gave them to the editor in chief, who translated them. But one day, my boss said, "You are too expensive! I have to pay you for your article and the editor in chief for his translation. Either you write in Spanish or you can no longer write for this magazine." So I rolled up my sleeves, placed the English-Spanish dictionary on my lap, and taught myself how to write in Spanish. And thanks to Elvira, I was able to continue developing my career as a journalist.

> *You mustn't rest on your laurels.*

Helen Gurley Brown

My first mentor was Elvira Mendoza, and she was hard on me, just like Helen Gurley Brown, my second mentor. I admire and respect strong and strict yet feminine women, like these two ladies. Elvira Mendoza was the epitome of beauty and elegance, a Colombian woman with red nail polish and perfectly coiffed black hair. She was simply gorgeous. She taught me how to be a strong woman and was my first journalism teacher. Helen Gurley Brown, *Cosmopolitan*'s editor in chief—a magazine that was already one hundred thirty years old when Helen began working there—was my work mother.

When Helen became *Cosmopolitan*'s editor in chief, she turned the magazine into a sexual freedom manual for women and spoke to them about sex just like *Playboy* talked to men about sex—this had never been done before. To some Latin American women, it was considered so risqué that when they read *Cosmo* at the hair salon, they made sure to hide the magazine's cover with another one so that no one could see what they were reading. They ate it up, but were embarrassed to openly admit it.

Then I dropped into Helen's life. She invented this new approach for *Cosmo*; however, my idea and direction for *Cosmopolitan en Español* had another angle. Rather than a sexual freedom manual, I wanted to turn it into a self-improvement guide for women. I believe the most important organ is above our neck and between our two ears, not between our legs. And I pushed my point of view into the magazine; however, Helen did not agree with this perspective. Her *Cosmopolitan* carried another message: She wanted the naive American girls to finally stand up and defend their right to an orgasm and sexuality. That was Helen, and she wanted to make sure this message was reflected in every *Cosmopolitan* edition around the world.

When I was named editor in chief at *Cosmopolitan en Español*, the company invited me and others who had received promotions to celebrate on an incredible yacht that sailed down the Hudson River and around the Statue of Liberty—an exquisite party with champagne and New York's crème de la crème. So there I was, a little Cuban woman who had just given birth (my daughter Titi was only a few months old), surrounded by this sophisticated group of people. I noticed Helen Gurley Brown and turned to *Cosmo*'s international director, Pat Miller, a fun-filled woman who loved drinking Bloody Marys. I asked Pat, "Hey, can that old lady fire me because I'm changing her magazine?" And Pat said, "No, she can't fire you." But Pat went and mentioned this to Helen and, a while later, Helen approached me. She was a petite but strong woman and spoke with a soft and sexy voice and didn't use underwear or bras. She suddenly grabbed my arm and I immediately assumed she was taking me somewhere to chat. However, I felt her fingers digging into my arm, and as this happened, she said with her delicate voice, "This old lady can't fire you, but she can make your life a living hell."

> *You can be tough as nails without losing your feminine touch.*

At the end of our relationship, before she passed away, she would sign all her letters to me "Mama." My work mother taught me that you can be tough as nails without losing your feminine touch. She also taught me endless lessons on women's sexuality that I was clueless about because I was a Cuban woman who'd gone to Catholic school all her life. I'm so lucky to have had her in my life; if not, I probably never would've married a man eleven years younger than me!

Celia Cruz and Gloria Estefan

I've just talked about my two professional mentors with you, two women who were my bosses and taught me so much about my career and my life. The other two people who served not only as my professional mentors, but my personal mentors, are my two best friends: Celia Cruz (who was one generation older than I am) and Gloria Estefan (one generation younger than I am). Since Celia's passing, I'm left with only Gloria, but I learned so much from both of them, including how to manage fame and how to maintain a happy marriage, one that has lasted for thirty years in a world where most couples don't even make it to a few.

Once, while I was having lunch with Celia, she noticed something was off with me. She was sitting next to me and asked what was wrong, and I answered, "I have this a@#*! talking crap about me. He's constantly throwing me under the bus at press time." Celia still carried a purse at the time—she later stopped doing so to protect her nails and used her husband as a personal purse. She'd put her makeup and all her other stuff in his pockets to avoid breaking a nail. She handed it to me and said, "Hold this for a second." The purse could have been bigger than Celia! She put her hand inside, pulled out some press clippings and showed them to me. "Look at these," she said. "This reporter says horrible things about me whenever he has the chance and I even go to his children's first communions because he will never know how much his words hurt me. Don't let them hurt you; don't let them know you are hurt." And that's

> *Let hurtful words fall on deaf ears.*

how I learned one of the most valuable lessons in my career: Let hurtful words fall on deaf ears.

Another time, Gloria realized I was down and, just like Celia, asked me what was the matter. I told her I thought I was depressed, and she quickly replied, "Careful, don't confuse depression with exhaustion. I've been extremely exhausted in the middle of a tour with endless dates and traveling plus nonstop promotional interviews, and I've been so tired I've found myself crying in the shower, but when I took a closer look, I realized I was just exhausted. You have to understand that in our careers sometimes the pressure and workload are inhumane, and we can easily confuse exhaustion with our state of mind." Gloria taught me how to stay strong at work.

Each one of these women has played a key role in my life. Their words, their advice, their voice of experience were my guides during decisive moments. I will never forget them and will always hold them close to my heart. A mentor marks you for life and inspires you to accomplish all your goals and dreams. Don't miss out on this amazing opportunity, and if you don't have a mentor handy, go out and find him or her. You will learn much more than you can imagine.

Knowledge Is Power

If you don't have a mentor, find one. Start at work and other organizations you belong to. You can also search online to learn how to find one. Remember: A mentor can be a boss, a professor, a friend, or a family member. Just make sure it is someone you admire and respect and someone who can teach you the skills you need to learn to get ahead.

Learn, Learn, Learn

I like learning more than sleeping, and that's saying a lot because I love to sleep. I like learning more than eating, and I'm a big eater. I even like learning more than sex . . . I *love* learning. When I read at night, I'm constantly hopping on Google to further explore what I'm reading about, because I want to learn more about what I just read, because I want even more information. Learning is as basic as breathing.

One of the best pieces of advice my mom ever gave me was the following: "Don't learn how to do what you don't like doing. If you learn how to make desserts, you will be making desserts for every family gathering. If you learn how to sew, you will sew everyone's clothes, like your grandmother. So, don't learn how to do what you don't like doing." I took this very seriously, so seriously that I am completely useless at home. I don't know how to cook, I don't clean, I don't take care of the household chores, and I'm totally aware of this decision, as I made it when I was twelve, after paying attention to my mom's wise words. On the flip side, I've focused my attention on learning everything I absolutely love doing. And I know that if I don't know how to do something, I'm capable of learning it. That's what I want for you.

> **Learning is the essence of life.**

Learning is the essence of life. It gives you knowledge, skills, conversation topics at gatherings; it inspires you. Never stop learning.

And look, when I talk about learning, I'm not referring to what you learn at school or college. Yes, education is extremely important in life, especially today when competition for top jobs is fierce. The more degrees you have under your belt, the better. However, are degrees absolutely necessary in order to be successful? No. Regardless of whether you go to school or not, if you want to educate yourself, you will. The only way to keep learning and growing is by staying abreast of your industry's innovations, reading, traveling, and inquiring. Never stop learning. However, it's important to note that lacking an education can turn your life into an uphill battle. Some people find their own success without formal training, but that doesn't work for everyone.

SHARING THE TRUTH

As I mentioned in chapter 1, while I was in college, my dad went bankrupt and he had to choose between paying for my education or my brother's. Being forced to leave college before graduating made me furious with my dad, even though I wasn't fond of going to school. But, in retrospect, this was the best thing that could have happened to me. Because of my father's decision, I realized that I could never depend on any man for money ever again. Rather than kill my appetite for learning, this change propelled me to become even smarter, more aggressive, and fully independent, paving the way for the person I am today.

I've learned so much from my job and colleagues, fans, guests, and audience members alike. *The Cristina Show* saved my life. It saved me from being frivolous and superficial, and it's helping me age better. Many of our shows not only taught others about the good and the bad in life, they taught me too. We learn from everything. I'm no longer afraid of growing old, which is something we all deal with as women—and as a vain Hispanic woman even more so. *The Cristina Show* fans are like family to me, so much so that when many of them approach me on the street, instead of asking for an autograph, they want a hug. And I give them that hug wholeheartedly because I am eternally grateful to them. I've learned more from them than they have from me. I wasn't the teacher. They were actually learning from the panelists and specialists on my show who shared their stories. I was the intermediary, and all the while I learned from both sides of the stage.

On the show, I also learned that I had to find common ground among the Latinos in the United States. This country still does not understand us. They categorize us into ethnic groups and that creates a great divide. So when I started the show, I began to think about the opposite concept: what unites us. We shared the same hardships and the desire for independence and freedom. So I approached my show with these common goals in mind, and I've applied them to many other projects since then. What you learn can later be applied in unimaginable ways. Be a sponge and soak up all the lessons and information headed your way.

Learning should be ever present in your life; however, there will come a time when you will be ready to share some of your life experiences and give advice to others. Teaching is just as important as learning, because if we share what we have learned, everyone's lives are enriched.

> *Teaching is just as important as learning, because if we share what we have learned, everyone's lives are enriched.*

The Apprentice Becomes the Mentor

With years of experience, having gone through life's ups and downs and all its lessons, there will come a time when you will be ready to teach. In the end, the apprentice becomes the mentor. When you reach this stage in your life, it is extremely important that you are ready and willing to share what you've learned with someone who needs it.

Mentors are essential to everyone's life. And now, as a mentor, you must learn how to choose your mentee. It is crucial that you choose your mentee wisely because you want someone next to you who really wants to be there. You will dedicate time and energy to your apprentice; therefore, choose someone who's ready to receive all this information, someone who has the potential to conquer his or her dreams. Keep in mind that apprentices, with their passion and appetite for life and success, can also surprise and inspire their mentors. It's a relationship that has the potential to benefit both parties if each is open to learning from the other.

Apprentices, with their passion and appetite for life and success, can also surprise and inspire their mentors.

Most of the people who have worked with me throughout the years, and through different stages, have managed to have their own careers with outstanding jobs and positions, and they all usually have one thing in common: They say that the time spent working with me—and I'm a tough boss with high demands—was where they learned the most. When they didn't believe in themselves because they were too young, I did it for them. And I literally pushed them against the wall to help them improve. I helped them discover their worth; I gave them the tools they needed to advance their careers, just like my mentors did for me. And I hope that one day they'll do the same for their apprentices.

PUT IT TO WORK FOR YOU!

1. Use the people who inspire you in life as a motivation to grow and learn from them.
2. Find a mentor.
3. If you don't know how to do something, don't be afraid to ask for help.
4. Never stop learning; it's as essential as breathing.
5. When the time comes, choose your apprentice carefully and share your knowledge so that we can all continue to learn and grow together.

5

Invest in Yourself

The best investment you can make in life is in yourself. Everything you invest in yourself will be reflected in all facets of your life. And what exactly does investing in yourself mean? It means investing money and time into the things that will help you get ahead in your personal and professional life. Invest in how you look, in what you wear, and in where you see yourself in the future. The investments you choose will depend on your goals, yet in every case and for every person, there are five basic things you should invest in to ensure a successful life:

1. Mind
2. Health
3. Image
4. Network
5. Team

If you know what you're worth and you invest in yourself, you can acquire the necessary tools and develop connections that will help you get ahead and stay on track.

When Marcos and I dared to construct our own TV studio

for *The Cristina Show*, we didn't do it so that I could become one of the four women in television history to own her own studio, and we also didn't do it so that I could become the first Latina to do it; we did it to invest in ourselves. People criticized and asked us why we had decided to take on such an expense, but we didn't even think twice. We saw it as an investment. And boy did it give us amazing results! For years, we used it to tape *The Cristina Show*, and now we rent it out to other TV shows and continue to receive profits from this excellent investment. By the same token, we were also criticized for investing in our personal team of publicists, consultants, and agents, but we didn't listen to the naysayers. You should invest a percentage of what you earn in your career to continue moving ahead and growing. That's what we were doing: investing in ourselves and in our future. And that's what I want you to do.

Invest in Your Mind

In chapter 4, we spoke about the importance of learning, and I want to emphasize this point again. Learning is one of the basic secrets to success; therefore, investing in your mind is essential. This type of investment spans both the creative and educational worlds. The idea is to develop your mental skills and keep up to date and informed in your field and the world around you.

Start by investing in your education. This includes but is not limited to advanced degrees, certificates, and even classes that will help you develop certain required skills in your industry—everything and anything that will help you climb your career ladder and get you to the top. You can register at a university and take in-class or online courses. And if you don't have money, there are still endless ways to continue learning. Let me give you one basic resource that many probably forget about: your city or town's public library. Registration is free and gives you access to an enormous world of books, audiobooks, DVDs, music, and periodicals, as well as events, classes, and speeches sponsored by the library. Besides, today many libraries also provide digital access to a great amount of literature. So if your excuse is that you don't have time to go to the library, then think about saving up and buying a tablet so you can access your library books online. Listen, when it comes to learning, there are no acceptable excuses.

Other options are to explore the conferences held in your city and take advantage of company or community classes. Search for educational TV shows and books that will help you develop your knowledge and skills. If you're curious about a particular subject, research it further. Everything you learn will be useful in your life; educating your mind is an investment that keeps on giving back.

Knowledge Is Power

A wonderful way to learn more from admirable and intelligent people is through TED Talks. TED is a nonprofit organization devoted to organizing conferences with the most fascinating thinkers and doers in the world, based on one main concept: Ideas Worth Spreading. Don't miss this fantastic opportunity to expand your mind. Here's the link: www.ted.com.

While working in women's magazines, I had learned that after thirty-five, women should start getting regular mammograms, and that's exactly what I did. (Today, it is said that this annual exam should begin after age forty.) That's why I was so taken aback when they found such a big undetected tumor: I had taken all of the necessary precautions prior to my surgery.

When you are scheduled for breast surgery, you must get a special, more detailed, mammogram as a precautionary measure. When I had my annual mammograms, I always told the woman who was examining me to also do an ultrasound because I have cystic breasts. That day, there was a new doctor, and when I told her she should do an ultrasound in addition to my mammogram, she insisted it wasn't necessary since my breasts were in good shape. Thinking back on this infuriated me more when that egg-sized tumor, which didn't show up in the mammogram, appeared out of nowhere. I should have insisted on the sonogram. Luckily, the tumor was benign. Thank God! If not, I would be telling quite a different story now.

Never ignore your health. Follow these simple and basic steps to ensure your physical well-being:

1. Get your annual checkups and pay your doctor a visit when you aren't feeling well.
2. Exercise on a weekly basis, at least three times a week.
3. Eat healthily, with a balanced diet and moderate portions.
4. Drink plenty of water and stay hydrated.
5. Don't forget to rest and sleep.

> ### Knowledge Is Power
>
> If you want to learn more about general health, both yours and your family's, check well-known online Web sites such as Medline Plus, a service of the U.S. National Library of Medicine and the National Institutes of Health: www.nlm.nih.gov/medlineplus. If you have specific questions or concerns regarding your health, please get professional help by going to your primary care physician.

Invest in Your Image

No matter what you do for work, your image plays an important role in career success. Don't think of this as being superficial. Your image is the first thing people will see, and it's important to make a great first impression, especially when it comes to meeting a potential employer or business connection. Although I personally believe that what you think is by far more important than what you wear, if you don't look the part, people won't take you seriously. In this world it's not enough to be it, you have to seem it.

Dressing for success is essential and to manage this you must be able to distinguish between what you would put on for a night on the town with friends and what you would wear to be taken seriously on the job. If you reveal your legs and cleavage, that's what your colleagues will look at. Remember these rules: If you're wearing a short skirt, don't wear a deep neckline. If you have a V neckline, wear a longer skirt or a pair of pants. Keep it professional, ladies.

SHARING THE TRUTH

Female executives who show too much skin are hurting themselves in the end because they will not be taken seriously. I'm not saying you have to dress like a nun, but you should control what you reveal at work. I'm not against women dressing sexy, you just have to know when and where to do it. The truth is men have a strong animal instinct and, even though we agree they should control it, they will inevitably be distracted by your legs or your cleavage if your look is too revealing, and while doing so they won't pay attention to what you have to contribute. I've been there; I know. Do you want respect? Then respect yourself and keep your breasts out of it; they're for your husband or partner.

When I began to ascend in the magazine world, I was very young—not yet thirty—and wore miniskirts and heels and my long hair down. I looked attractive, but whenever I went to the conference room for a meeting or tried to say something firmly and seriously as the editor of the magazine, the response I got from the men was usually, "Oh, you look so cute when you get angry." What? That infuriated me! I thought it was completely disrespectful. I wanted to be taken seriously. Finally, one day I decided to make a small change in how I looked. I tied my hair back in a ponytail, bought knee-length skirts, and wore glasses to look more respectable. And boy did it work! The key was that I stopped looking like I was flirting with them, and that's how the men began to respect me.

Your image should be directly linked to your career. Picture some classic professional roles, like that of a lawyer or musician, and note how easy it usually is to differentiate each one at first sight by what they're wearing. That's when you'll understand how this affects your career. Your image says a lot about you. For example, my two daughters have very different careers: Titi is a banker and Stephanie a fashion designer. Both dress for success, but what they wear is completely different. You shouldn't go to work at a bank dressed like a hippie. Titi goes

> *No matter what you do, no matter what your budget, always strive to look your best.*

to a store and buys two professional suits and several shirts to look respectable at work. Meanwhile, Stephanie designs what she wears. If she were to show up at work in a suit, her coworkers probably wouldn't take her too seriously as a fashion designer.

You have to know your audience. This isn't true only in the entertainment world. No matter what you do, you have an audience that depends on the role you want to play. Every industry has a uniform. It's up to you to see what that uniform is and how to adapt it to fit your position and career, so you can be taken seriously. No matter what you do, no matter what your budget, always strive to look your best. Having said this, you don't need to look like the rest of the herd. Add personal touches to make the look your own. You don't need to be a fashion victim. It's a fine balance, and to maintain it, you must learn how to choose clothes that favor your body shape. If something fits well, you will feel well, and that energy will be interpreted as self-confidence (a key to success that I will get into later, in chapter 10, "Know Your

Worth and Ask for What You Deserve"). When it comes to build-ing confidence, everything, right down to your clothes, counts.

To find the clothes that fit and make you feel good, you must figure out what type of body you have and what style looks best on you. If you aren't sure, check out the people you admire at work and note how they dress and present themselves. Cut out looks you like from magazines, use your cell phone to take photos of clothes that inspire you. Once you've chosen a professional look you like and feel you can identify with, try on different pieces and see what's most comfortable and what looks good on you. If you aren't sure, take pictures of yourself wearing different looks or ask a friend for help—make sure to choose someone who won't be afraid to tell you the truth. If you do this, you'll slowly learn how to find what looks good on you and what best rep-resents you in your career path, which will give you more self-confidence and, in turn, this will be reflected in all you do.

I've been down this road. I had to make changes to adapt to the different positions within my career. As I mentioned earlier, the first time I actively changed my image was when I swapped my personal look for a more professional one to be taken more seriously in the magazine industry. I later had to make another switch when I began working in television. When you are the "talent" on TV, the camera and light crew talk about you as if you aren't even a person with feelings, as if you were a piece of furniture. "Move her over there. Bring that light up so we don't see her wrinkles." Since I came from a world where I had been the boss, this treatment was totally new to me, and I felt it was completely disrespectful. Yet, I understood I was in a new world, and I would have to adjust to it.

Television is a visual medium and I was exposing myself to the camera lens for the first time at forty-one years old. I knew I had to invest in my body and how I looked, since both were now essential factors to my career. So, aside from losing weight, I decided to visit an amazing plastic surgeon in Los Angeles. He performed plastic surgery on my neck, gave me a facelift (the only one I've ever had done), and added a chin implant. When I got back to Miami, my dad wouldn't speak to me. He said I didn't look like myself, nor did I have any of the family features. But each time I passed by a mirror, I did a double take because I couldn't believe that was me; the surgeon did a fantastic job. Surgery is God's gift to humanity, unless you push it too far and become the Queen of Botox, like in Hollywood, where everyone looks like they're related. These touch-ups gave me the self-confidence I needed to appear on TV on a daily basis.

After I lost weight and looked better than before (by TV standards), I then decided to invest in Evie, a personal stylist from New York. I didn't hire her to tell me what my look should be. I had a clear picture of how I wanted to be portrayed, and I broke it down for her. I wanted to be taken seriously, I wanted clothes that connected to my current stage in life, so I told her I wanted to look like a Washington, D.C., lawyer, like Hillary Clinton. I'm a grown woman, and that's how I wanted to be seen. That was another investment I made in myself to benefit my career. For my daily talk show, we recorded two episodes a day, and I couldn't wear the same clothes. I've never really been interested in fashion, so I knew I needed help to create and maintain the image I wanted to portray on TV. Evie was excellent at her job and she knew the top New York designers, so she'd send me clothes for the entire month, and that wardrobe fit well and made me feel confident. I'm not trying to tell you that you must go get work done on your face or hire a personal stylist to be successful in *your* life. I'm just sharing my experience to show you that each position and every industry requires specific investments in yourself. You must figure out how to invest in your image to gain more respect so that you can come out on top in whatever you set out to do.

Invest in Your Network

During my years as editor in chief at *Cosmopolitan en Español*, I was the youngest woman to hold that position in Latin America, and I knew I had to invest in my connections in order to create and maintain a solid network. So, when my friend and sales director, Rocío, and I traveled to Mexico on business, we hosted enormous lunches to create and cultivate personal relationships with each one of our clients. Today, that human connection is getting lost among the social media commotion and I think we need to bring it back. You must invest in your network. Throw a dinner for your colleagues, organize a cocktail hour for people in your industry, invite someone you admire and respect to dinner, find out what events are suitable within your industry and create and nurture your professional network by hosting one. This is a key investment in your future.

I have a friend who's an old-school publicist and every year she hosts a Christmas party for her clients in her own home. This way, besides being in touch with them throughout the year, she also makes sure to nurture a personal relationship with each one. By developing these relationships, when the time comes to choose someone with whom to work on a new project, guess who they'll call first?

There are several ways to invest in your network, depending on your industry, but many just don't take this initiative anymore. Host a holiday party, like my publicist friend. Put together a cocktail hour at a bar or organize a special lunch, and pay for it yourself. Choose a place with a style and ambiance that matches your industry. (Go for more of a classic vibe if you're a lawyer or banker, and more bohemian if you're in the arts.) Invite the key people you'd like to develop closer business ties with, including clients and possible future clients. People don't usually think about hosting these types of events because they use their extra money to go on vacation. Don't get me wrong, vacations are also important, but you must set aside a certain percentage of your income to invest in yourself and get ahead in your career. Taking the initiative to plan one of the previously mentioned activities could make your boss notice you or a client give you more work. The confidence you display by hosting one of these events lets those around you—your bosses, your colleagues, and your clients—know that you are capable of taking the bull by its horns and becoming a leader. When opportunity knocks, answer the door! You'll win some and lose some, but don't be afraid to take the plunge.

> *When opportunity knocks, answer the door! You'll win some and lose some, but don't be afraid to take the plunge.*

Investing in yourself can be incredibly rewarding. Take Marcos, for example. When he decided to leave the Miami Sound Machine to be closer to us, his family, it was a huge life change, one that I will forever thank him for making. By taking this plunge, he had to invest in himself to move his career into the next stage. He not only grew his network, he also transformed networking and public relations into a successful business and founded his company, Magic City Media. In the eighties, Latinos still did not see the need for this type of service. Many wondered why they needed to spend money on promoting themselves if they were already famous. The key lies in the word "spend." They didn't realize that this wasn't an expense, but rather an investment. By investing in their public relations, they would be able to reach a wider audience and move their successful career to the next level. The same can be said about your life: If you invest in your network, you will be able to develop important relationships with your bosses, colleagues, and clients, people who in the future may help you grow and reach the successful life you so desire.

Invest in Your Team

Investing in your team at work and in your community is another essential step toward success. We must be supportive and generous with others; that good energy will attract only more good energy to your life. The first step is to create a team of people who are smart, resourceful, hardworking, and as passionate as you are.

> *We must be supportive and generous with others; that good energy will attract only more good energy to your life.*

I know many people who never hire those more intelligent than they are because they fear they could steal their jobs. Throughout my professional career, I've done quite the contrary. I've always made it a point to surround myself with bright and intelligent people. And if one of them knows how to do something better than I do, welcome aboard! Teamwork strengthens our talent; therefore, envious and insecure people are not welcome in my group. Envy is the soul's cancer. To be envious is the same as watching from the sidelines instead of keeping your eyes on the goal ahead. While you're investing energy in envying someone for something, you're losing precious time that should be used to focus on your own dreams; instead of getting closer to your goals, you begin to leave them behind. We need to support each other to get ahead and avoid envy at all costs. One person's success within my team is celebrated by all of us. Besides, you never know where that person may end up with their success. In the future, you may find you have to ask that person for help or for a job, so it's essential to foster positive relationships and invest in your team.

During my magazine years, I was the woman with sixteen freelance jobs. I did everything I possibly could to continue nurturing my career and getting ahead. And, to do so, I needed to be able to count on a good team. For example, I was given a specific budget to produce twenty-six special issues a year, so I used that budget to offer my magazine employees freelance work to increase their incomes. They were grateful for the opportunity, and I was happy to help them and to count on their help. When the magazine workday came to a close, we shifted gears and focused on our freelance work till eleven p.m.

I applied this same idea during my years in television. My TV employees were paid by the network, but they were all loyal to me. Why? Well, one of the things Marcos and I did as an incentive was to give our employees a Christmas bonus or gift, and we organized theme-based contests where the winner could go home with cash—in some cases up to two thousand dollars. This all came directly from our pockets. Another way we motivated them was by taking them out to dinner or hosting some sort of celebration each time we ended a taping cycle. We also established sushi and tequila nights that became very popular with our work team and our show's guests. We knew it was key to invest in our team to show them our appreciation and create a bond that would benefit all of us. You must fight for your people. It's important to

> *You must fight for your people.*

have your team's loyalty and for them to know whom they work for on a deeper level; it's an essential part of being a good boss.

That's why I recommend you invest not only in yourself but also in those who surround and support you. When you do things from the heart, with good intentions, at some point, out of the blue, an unexpected door could open and lead you to another project that had never crossed your mind. This has happened to me many times.

No matter how far you get in life, never lose the ability to listen to those around you. Part of investing in them is giving them some of your time. You will be surprised by what you can learn and who you can learn from, even those you least expect, if you stay open to this possibility. The wisest advice could come from the guy who cuts your lawn. When you believe you're a hotshot, you lose connection with reality. Remember: You never know who may give you a word of advice that will fill you with the inspiration and hope you needed in that very moment. Surround yourself with good people who lift your spirit and invest in them as well as in yourself. That way, everybody wins.

PUT IT TO WORK FOR YOU!

1. Invest a percentage of your income and time in yourself to continue to grow and succeed in your career and life.
2. Exercise your mind. Learning is one of the basic secrets to success, so invest in your mind and develop not only your intellect but also your creativity.
3. Make your health a priority. Get your annual checkups, eat a balanced and healthy diet, exercise, and sleep. Without health, there is no life.
4. Dress for success. The way you choose to look reflects who you are.
5. Invest in your network to develop a personal relationship with your bosses, colleagues, and clients, and never forget to invest in your team. Being supportive and generous with others will attract only good energy into your life.

6

Create Your Own Campaign

etworking is one of the basic investments you must make in yourself, as we clearly discussed in the previous chapter. Now, I want you to not only invest in yourself, I want you to campaign for yourself. We must all get on the campaigning trail to advance our careers and open new doors to success. You never know when or where opportunity will come knocking at your door. That's why I'm a firm believer that you should not only network within your industry, but also attend events related to causes or issues you care about.

> *You never know when or where opportunity will come knocking at your door.*

When Marcos and I began campaigning for ourselves, we called it "breaking new markets," which means traveling to meet people and promote yourself in person, much like political campaigns. We wanted to make *The Cristina Show* a hit in as many markets as possible, so we took our own money and invested in a public relations campaign to open new doors. Univision's PR department was focused on the network, not each individual show, and I aspired to have a show with high ratings on a national level. So, like many politicians on the campaign trail, I decided to go to cities and places where the network didn't have a strong presence, and connect directly with the people in these areas as a way of breaking into these new markets.

We didn't have much money at the time, but what little we did have we used to pay for flights. We took Miguel, my makeup artist, along with us so he could paint my "Cristina face," and I made free appearances. We were like The Three Musketeers, "all for one and one for all," because it all came out of our pocket. The goal was to take part in local events within these specific communities so I could become part of them. We ended up in the most unlikely places and situations, such as participating in local parades with me perched up on top of the craziest floats. But investing in that campaign paid off. We broke into these markets and our ratings skyrocketed.

So, again, don't rest on your laurels. Don't wait for events and offers to magically come to you. Get out of your comfort zone and connect with more people. Go to local and national events and conferences, even venture into international territory, and campaign for yourself. The more people you know, the more opportunities will come your way.

Knowledge Is Power

When you go out on your own campaign trail, don't forget to bring along enough business cards to hand out to every person you meet. You can get them made online or at your local office supply store. Also, make sure you keep the cards you receive in a safe place, and the day after the event, send a personal e-mail to each one of your new contacts to establish the new connection.

Campaign Within and Beyond Your Industry

Don't just network in your industry. Cross-pollinate. In other words, no matter what industry you're in, campaign in other ones too. Find causes that you're interested in or care about, such as organizations that support women in the workforce or fight against AIDS, and also campaign for yourself in those events. Cross-pollinating is like that concept of putting all your eggs in more than one basket. Open your mind and your campaign trail to other industries, interests, and causes. Go above and beyond your work world.

Creating a social network and putting yourself out there is not only one of the main secrets to a successful career, it will also lead to a successful life. In Marcos's words, when you're fishing, sometimes you have to venture out into the deep sea to find the big fish because they aren't close to shore. You may think some of your efforts or trips were somewhat useless, but then, out of nowhere, something incredible and unexpected may come from one of these events and bring an even greater reward.

> *When you're fishing, sometimes you have to venture out into the deep sea to find the big fish because they aren't close to shore.*

For example, what truly opened a ton of doors for me was when I became involved in other organizations outside of my industry, such as amfAR (The American Foundation for AIDS Research), an international nonprofit organization dedicated to AIDS research, prevention, and education.

After being on air with *The Cristina Show* for five years, my show's supervising producer at the time, Jorge Insua, approached me and asked, "What else do you want to be involved in outside of the show?" And I immediately replied that the cause I was most interested in was AIDS and AIDS education. Jorge's question could not have been timelier. Once I became famous, it seemed like everyone and their mother was asking for money for their organizations, or what I used to call "the illness of the week." Instead of spreading my money thin among several causes, I thought that choosing one close to my heart was the right way to go about it.

I went with amfAR because I truly cared about the cause and the young people that the disease mainly affected. Life was different during my younger years. People could be intimate and have sex without having to worry about diseases like AIDS. When AIDS became an epidemic, the public was oblivious to the nature of the disease. A lot of my fans and audience members would ask me how the disease was passed on, asking questions like, "Can you get it through French kissing?" The lack of information caused widespread panic and paranoia.

I became amfAR's Hispanic spokesperson and we contributed one of the largest donation of the year: fifty thousand dollars. And guess how I raised it? While on tour, campaigning, I signed autographs and sold each one for a dollar. Campaigning for myself outside of my industry opened up a gigantic door into another world that I had no idea was within my reach: I flew to New York, where I met Elizabeth Taylor, to launch the amfAR campaign in Spanish and have our photos taken together. We also traveled together to Washington, D.C., and I later spoke

SHARING THE TRUTH

Sexually transmitted diseases affect everyone, especially young people, so education and prevention became my cause. Through my show and the discussions we initiated, we armed people with the information they needed to protect themselves and make educated decisions. However, when I spoke about certain subjects, like sex, my audience would react with comments such as, "You can't talk about sex in a daytime show when children are at home," to which I would respond, "I'm talking about sex for the children, not for you."

with Elizabeth at the United Nations. "I'm the lady who fights AIDS in Spanish," was how I introduced myself.

Another example of how stepping outside of my industry helped expand my world is Casa Cristina. I began receiving calls from companies asking to launch a product line with my name on it. I'm not too interested in clothes, but I love to decorate. So, I told Marcos, "Let's create a home decor line." We designed furniture, rugs, lamps, home accessories, bed linens; you could furnish and decorate your entire home with our products. And it was a huge success. As a bonus, I was the first Latina to create this type of line. I went from being the Latin Oprah to the Latin Martha Stewart.

Of all the things I've done in my career, Casa Cristina is the one I miss most because I truly enjoyed designing the pieces. If I could, I would definitely do it again. And I'm proud of what my team and I accomplished. By opening myself to this new venture and challenging myself to apply my creative skills, I was able to turn my passion for decoration into a successful business. Infinite possibilities await you, if you dare to step outside your comfort zone.

> *Infinite possibilities await you, if you dare to step outside your comfort zone.*

From a Personal to a Presidential Campaign

I don't like politics. I come from a Communist country and saw what can happen within a corrupt political system. But I also learned the importance of voting. If we don't vote, things never change. By voting, you can affect the change you want to see. If you have the option to vote, always exercise that right, even more so as a woman. Voting is equivalent to having a voice and exercising our right to be heard. So when the president of the United States knocked on my door, asking for my help with the Hispanic vote, I decided to welcome this new unexpected opportunity and see where it might take me.

When we received the call from President Barack Obama's team in May 2012, they told us they knew the Hispanic vote would be the decisive one in the next U.S. presidential election and they wanted my help.

They asked me to join President Obama's campaign and be their Hispanic spokesperson. I hated politics due to everything I had endured with Fidel Castro. Because of him and in the name of politics, my family had to flee from Cuba. So my initial answer was no. Besides, at first I wasn't really convinced that I liked Obama. When I saw him speak, I noticed he used many words in his speeches that I had already heard as a little girl. At times, it was like listening to Fidel Castro and Hugo Chávez, and that made me extremely uncomfortable; I felt he was a demagogue.

One day, the president himself called me on the phone and I was completely honest with him: "I don't know you. I know Hillary Clinton, I've worked with her, I know Bill Clinton, and I know the Bush family, but I don't know you. So, if I don't meet you and can't see your eyes and observe how you are and if you're sincere or not, I'm not going to get involved in this because I don't like politics." And I went on to explain that I come from a Communist country and all things related to that experience. But he insisted. He asked me to give him an opportunity to meet in person. At the end of the conversation, I said, "Mr. President, I can't wait to shake your hand." And he answered, "No, but what about a hug and a kiss?" and then I thought, *Ah, this guy is okay.* We met in Miami and shared a funny moment. The president is very tall, while Marcos and I are quite the opposite, so, when we met that first time, we looked like two shorties with him in the middle. When we finally had the chance to talk, and I was able to see who President Obama was, I changed my mind.

Another reason why I agreed to help President Obama's campaign was because he is African-American. I come from a country with many mulattoes. Actually, my mulatto blood is right in my butt, because I'm Spanish and mulatto. In Cuba, we saw dreadful things happen, but racism was not one of them. I first encountered racism as an issue when we moved to the United States.

We arrived in June 1960 and brought our beloved nanny with us—she was black and her name was Idalia. She had all of us blond kids under her care. When we first got on a bus in Miami, the driver told her she couldn't sit with us. She had to sit at the back of the bus, but she couldn't do this because she couldn't lose sight of us. So she'd get hysterical each time that happened. She made us get off the bus immediately, unable to comprehend this racism, which she had never experienced in our home country. And that wasn't the only problem she encountered; she couldn't go to the same bathroom as us or drink from the same fountain. We fell smack in the middle of the racial divide when we arrived in this country, so I understood the meaning behind this amazing step forward of having an African-American president in a country where only fifty years ago, he wouldn't have been able to sit next to me on a bus. I began taping a series of ads in Spanish for President Obama's campaign, which were, thank God, very successful. However, problems followed. Some of my fellow Cubans in Miami began to criticize me for supporting the Obama campaign. In the airports, they would yell out names at me, like "traitor" and "communist." Meanwhile, we had agreed that I would do the campaign ads, but would not participate in press conferences or speeches. I have always said I do not have a connection between my brain and my mouth and I didn't want to inadvertently say something that would in any way harm the president's reelection. Then came the conference call regarding the Democratic National Convention. I made it clear that I wasn't interested in giving a speech, but they wanted me to participate on a more personal level. They wanted my presence to have an important role at the convention. During the call, Jim

Messina—the president's campaign director—suddenly spoke directly to me and asked me to give a speech at the Democratic National Convention, and without thinking twice about it, I instantly replied, "Yes." Everyone was surprised with my immediate response, including me. But I had no doubts. That "yes" came from the heart.

On the day of the convention, Jorge Insua—the president of Marketing and Development for my company—grabbed me by the hand and accompanied me to the wings of the stage. I think he was afraid I would run for the hills, but it was quite the contrary. When I saw that mass of people, I suddenly broke into a little jog while heading to the microphone, in the center of the stage. Once I reached the podium, I noticed the teleprompter was stuck. Thankfully, with my years of TV experience, I was able to improvise while, backstage, Jorge ran around asking for someone to please fix the teleprompter. Only a few seconds went by, and when I finally saw everything on screen, I took a deep breath and dove in. The president's team had approved my speech, although a few improvised phrases (in Spanish!) did escape my mouth; I couldn't help it. The energy of the twenty-five thousand people in that arena applauding and cheering me on was electrifying.

In my speech, I mentioned what it was like to come to the United States with my family at twelve years old as a Cuban exile, to the land of the free, where if you work very hard anything is possible. I shared how, after having to leave college because I couldn't afford it, I turned my internship into a job and that job into a business and a TV show that at one point had one hundred million viewers in forty countries. The audience cheered and applauded, and I enthusiastically responded, *"¡Si se puede!"* (Yes we can!), which fired them up even more. On that amazing day, I said that, to me, the American Dream is not just a dream but a promise and the story of my life and that of the DREAMers, and for the first time that promise was in danger in the hands of Governor Romney. His plan was going to move us backward, and what I truly hoped to express to the public was that we had to move forward, and in order to do so, we had to reelect President Obama. I got on that stage because I wanted to help keep that American promise alive and pass it on to my children and grandchildren, and to all young people striving to make their dreams a reality.

When I turned to leave, people started yelling, *"¡Viva Cuba!"* (Long live Cuba!) and I replied, *"¡Pa'lante!"* (Forward!). Usually, convention guest speakers are very local and somewhat repetitive, and the audience gets bored. So, when I got on that stage, I gave them my all and yelled *"Pa'lante!"* and delivered my speech. The audience went wild. As soon as I finished, feeling accomplished, I was heading off the stage when I heard a huge roar from the crowd. It sounded like an enormous wave breaking onshore, and when I turned toward the stage I had just left behind and looked at the audience in the arena, I saw that everyone out there was on their feet. I couldn't believe it. I had never felt such a thrilling sensation before in my life. It was amazing.

Although I don't like giving speeches, that experience truly moved me and I would do it again in a heartbeat. I felt so much love and acceptance, and I learned that sometimes we say no to things out of fear, and we unknowingly limit ourselves, shutting the door on an opportunity that could give back so much, if we just have the guts to take the risk and do it. That day, I spoke in front of twenty-five thousand people and millions more, mainly English-speaking Americans, who were watching on TV! I didn't even think about it, I just went for it and got it done. If I had stopped to think about it, fear would've taken hold and I wouldn't have been able to go through with it.

Knowledge Is Power

If you'd like to see this speech, go to the following link: http://youtube/ajXs15hh-hw. And don't miss seeing Benita Veliz's speech, which is at the beginning of the video clip. Benita is a young Mexican woman who, as a little girl, arrived in San Antonio, Texas, with her family in search of a better life. She graduated from high school at sixteen at the top of her class, and four years later she graduated with a double major from college. In 2012, Benita made history by being the first undocumented person to speak at a political national convention. Her story is incredibly inspiring and an example of what it means to persevere, work hard, and never give up.

To conquer a fear, you have to face it head-on because if you try to avoid it, you'll inevitably have to face it later. You would think I couldn't be afraid of speaking in public given my long career as a TV host. But the thing is, when you work in TV, you're actually talking to a hole in a camera. There are millions of people watching you, but you don't see them. It's not like actually having thousands of people, who don't necessarily know who you are, watching you live. It took me a while to overcome that fear, but today I can even enjoy public speaking. I've noticed that when I'm listening to someone give a bad speech, I feel like grabbing the mike and saying, "That's not how it's done." But it's clear that it was a fear I had to face and overcome in order to be where I am today. We all have fears, but we cannot let them paralyze us. Go ahead, face them, it's worth it; once you overcome at least one of them, you will feel stronger and more self-confident. Rise up and shine!

> *We all have fears, but we cannot let them paralyze us. Rise up and shine!*

I'm still involved in some campaigns, such as one supporting The Affordable Care Act, but I would never accept a political position. To me, politics has always seemed like a profession where ambition and power eclipse good intentions. I don't like to take political positions, but I do believe we must support political causes, because if you don't vote and let your voice be heard, then our rights can be easily taken away, just like what happened in Cuba when Fidel and communism took over.

I've actually always been involved in social issues, campaigning through my show for causes such as organ donation, affordable medical insurance, AIDS, gay marriage. Each one of these issues, in some way or other, involves politics. Furthermore, I've had to campaign for myself every single day of my career and life. Politicians do it every four years, but I do it every day—it's called *ratings*. And just like in politics, the time you last on air depends on your fans. As long as they feel you're doing something important for them, you will still be there. If they feel that you are doing something that benefits you instead of them, your time is up. So, whatever you decide to do for yourself, make sure it has a bigger purpose, that you do it for reasons other than just for personal gain.

PUT IT TO WORK FOR YOU!

1. Don't wait for opportunities to magically appear at your door. Take action and go to local, national, and international events, and campaign for yourself.

2. Campaign for yourself inside and outside your industry. You never know where your next big break may come from.

3. Become involved in a cause or nonprofit organization. Open your world to new opportunities.

4. Conquer your fears, face them head-on, and you'll see that you will come out of it a winner.

5. Make sure you have a bigger purpose in life and that your campaign goes beyond simply focusing on your own personal gain.

7

Toot Your Own Horn

At this point, I've already expressed the importance of investing in yourself and of campaigning for yourself. Now you must exercise the third key step: You've got to toot your own horn. Yes, you read that right. If you've already invested in yourself and have gone out on the campaign trail, well, now's the time to stop being modest and feel sufficiently confident to toot your own horn. If you know you're good at doing something in particular, don't be afraid to shout it from the rooftops.

I recently had a conversation with my makeup artist, Miguel, and I asked him: "Who's the best makeup artist in Miami?"

"Me," he answered with absolutely no hesitation.

"I know that, do you?" I responded.

"Yes, I'm the best. That's why my fee is what it is and I do what I do," he said.

"And do you say this to people?" I asked.

"Of course, that's why they hire me! And I have it on my Web site, where I also list all my accomplishments."

Miguel is tooting his own horn and he has every right. He's an excellent makeup artist, and if he didn't speak up and say it openly in front of his clients or on his Web site, people might

> *If you don't believe in yourself, the rest of the world won't either.*

not have the chance find out. As a client, seeing his self-confidence in what he does makes you feel you are in good hands. And he follows through with action, because the results speak for themselves.

No matter what you do, you have to aspire to be the best, know it, and say it. Believe in yourself. If you don't believe in yourself, the rest of the world won't either. When you shine with self-confidence, others take notice. As women, it's even more important for us to break the tradition of being modest, which we're taught from a young age, and openly say that we're the best at what we do. Don't be afraid. It doesn't matter what other people think, this is for you. If you don't toot your own horn, if you don't let your achievements be known, if you don't make people hear and respect you, you can bet someone else will take the credit from you. The world is built on competition, so you must learn how to speak highly of yourself at the right time to promote your skills and accomplishments.

While growing up, many of us were told that we had to be modest and well mannered, which meant no bragging in public. When you receive a compliment, instead of smiling, looking down, and pretending you don't deserve it, do the contrary. Look the person straight in the eye and say "Thank you." You know you deserve that compliment, that acknowledgment, that praise, so accept and enjoy it! I want to make one thing crystal clear: Tooting your own horn does not mean that you are rude. Saying you are the best at what you do is not a bad thing.

Stop thinking that a "refined lady" must never talk about

SHARING THE TRUTH

Throughout my career, before going up onstage to receive an award, Marcos always says to me: "Please, please be modest," because modesty is not in my nature. What I do, I do well, and I know it. I know I'm very good at my job the same way I know that I can't fry an egg. Therefore, I'm not afraid to toot my own horn and accept awards with gratitude, knowing that I deserve them. These awards and acknowledgments are the result of all the effort, passion, and perseverance that I put into my career. And if someone says it's all going to your head and you're full of yourself, use my response: "I'm not full of myself, I am me." I don't care what others think of me, what matters is what *I* think of myself. Don't be afraid to toot your own horn. You deserve it.

herself with such self-confidence; instead, learn how to sing your own praises simply because you deserve it.

Accept Your Strengths and Your Weaknesses

Before tooting your own horn you must discover and accept your strengths and weaknesses. In chapter 2, I urged you to find what you are passionate about. During that search, you probably also encountered things that don't hold your interest or that you don't like doing. We all have things we do well and others that we don't. You can't toot your own horn about something that you can't put your heart and soul into, because if you do, nobody will take you seriously. Remember: We all have limits, and part of blowing our own horns is recognizing that we're not perfect. Do not aspire to perfection—it's limiting, rigid, and unrealistic: Nobody is perfect.

For example, I know I'm excellent in my career; and I'm a fantastic wife, mother, and grandmother; but if you make me do house chores, I'm useless. I don't mind saying it out loud. Recognizing your weaknesses brings a positive balance into your life. Knowing you are the best at something and being able to openly say it demonstrates the type of self-confidence that is essential in life.

Learn How to Say You Are the Best at What You Do

Once you've recognized your weaknesses, focus on nurturing and building up your strengths. Then, talk yourself up and toot that horn; if you don't do it, no one will do it for you. Have enough self-confidence to firmly say that you can do the job and you can do it better than anyone else. And then follow through with action. Words are useless if they aren't supported by action. If you toot your own horn by saying you're incredibly punctual, but day after day, you're always more than ten minutes late, you are not what you say you are. This can be applied in any area of your life. There's a reason why this famous saying exists: "Actions speak louder than words."

When actions back your words, why not say you are the best at what you do? The best example I've seen is Celia Cruz. Do you know how much work it took for Celia to get to where she got as a black woman? She worked nonstop, she succeeded, and she died a legend. She knew she was a legend while still alive

Knowledge Is Power

Following your words with actions is so crucial that plenty of other phrases were created to further emphasize the importance of action:

- "Deeds are fruits, words are but leaves."
- "Easier said than done."
- "Talk is cheap when words have no value."
- "Words are mere bubbles of water, but deeds are drops of gold."
- "All talk and no action."

Choose the one you like the most and apply it to your life. Words and promises come alive with action.

and had no problem accepting it and tooting her own horn for all her hard work and success.

Celia was wonderful. When she came on my show as a guest, after the taping she would stand outside in the parking lot and, as the audience left the set, she'd stretch out her arms and say: "Touch me, touch me, touch me." She knew she deserved the people's love, just like she knew that she would be no one without her fans. Many other artists that came on my show, most just one-hit wonders, immediately asked me where the audience exited the building, so they could leave through another exit and avoid being bothered by them. But not Celia, nor Gloria. They are true superstars.

Positive Reinforcement

Giving and accepting positive reinforcement is as important as receiving and giving constructive criticism. Positive reinforcement is motivating and helps you stay on the right track. And just as we like to receive it, we must also give it to others.

It's important to use positive reinforcement with those around you, from your family and friends to your colleagues and clients. This gesture helps build self-confidence. Obviously, this reinforcement is not free. If you're not doing something well, you must be equally open to receiving constructive criticism. You don't have to demoralize people while explaining what they ought to improve. The idea isn't to simply highlight what they are doing wrong, but also to offer help so that they can find ways to improve. And, once they do improve, congratulate and motivate them to keep at it. Positive reinforcement helps us reach that moment when we deserve to toot our own horn.

Acknowledgment

I don't enjoy working just for the sake of work. I like well-paid work and having people give me credit for what I do. I believe that for everyone recognition isn't just flattering, it's important. Acknowledgments are important for you, for your self-esteem, but also for those who employ you, as well as for the direction in which you want to move. For example, do you think I would've been called to speak at the Democratic National Convention if President Obama hadn't seen all my awards and acknowledgments? An award or public acknowledgment opens more doors and gives you the chance to get a better job or a raise. And it's just as important to give out acknowledgment. Acknowledge your employees and those who help you be where you are today.

> *An award or public acknowledgment opens more doors and gives you the chance to get a better job or a raise.*

That's what we did with our Univision contests—the ones where we would give the staff incentives to come up with the best show ideas. Those contests served to motivate our employees and to share the success we had achieved as a team. Without them, the show couldn't have happened. Each person had to fulfill his or her part for everything to run smoothly. By creating those contests and handing out cash prizes that came from our own pockets, we were sharing our successes and acknowledging the role our employees had in helping us get that far.

In 1999, when the Hollywood Chamber of Commerce honored me with a star on the Hollywood Walk of Fame, I wanted to celebrate it with my loved ones. I invited my entire family to come with me. What I wanted most was to share this acknowledgment with them because they were all a part of the hard work that led to this accomplishment. In that moment, I wasn't just tooting my own horn, I was tooting it for my entire family. So remember, toot your own horn, don't be afraid to say you are the best at what you do, but also share your success with those around you, the people who have supported and helped you reach this high point in your life.

PUT IT TO WORK FOR YOU!

1. No matter what you do, you must aspire to be the best, know it, and say it.

2. Don't aim for perfection, accept your weaknesses and focus on your strengths in order to succeed.

3. Back your words with actions so that you are taken seriously and respected.

4. Give and receive positive reinforcement to create a stronger sense of confidence in yourself and others.

5. Aspire to receive awards and acknowledgments for what you do, and don't forget to acknowledge those around you. Acknowledgment is not only flattering, it's important.

8

Never Give Up

Here are the three basic secrets for success in life:

1. Never give up.
2. Never, never give up.
3. And never, never, never give up.

It's that simple. If you fall down, pick yourself back up. *Forward and Onward, don't ever look back not even to gain momentum!* I've used this phrase in Spanish *(¡Pa'lante, pa'lante; pa'trás ni pa' coger impulso!)* throughout my career, and what it really means is that even if you fall down, even if you lose, even if you feel destroyed, like I did when *The Cristina Show* was canceled after twenty-one years of hard work, loyalty, and success, well, there's nowhere to go but up and you must keep moving forward. Never give up. I've experienced it in the flesh, and now I'm sharing my story with you so that you can learn from my life experiences. No matter how many doors are slammed in my face, I will never give up, because I'm the one responsible for making my dreams a reality. If I give up, who else will fight for

> *Don't ever let anyone or anything destroy you.*

them? It's not only my motivation; it's my responsibility. I hope that you will apply this rule in your own life too. Don't ever let anyone or anything destroy you.

The Shocking End of *The Cristina Show*

Univision was very good to me while I worked there, but I was also very good to them. And when I say "them," I'm not talking about the network. Univision is not a logo or a building; it's made up of the people who work there. What makes Univision the number one Spanish-language network in the United States are the people who were there from the beginning, the ones who made it their lives, like my producer, like myself, like Don Francisco, María Elena Salinas, Jorge Ramos, Lili Estefan, Raúl "El Gordo" de Molina, María Antonieta Collins, Neida Sandoval, and Teresa Rodríguez. Great people make a company great. If you use English-language networks as an example, Walter Cronkite developed his career at CBS, and Barbara Walters at ABC. They are both national icons and stewards of broadcast journalism, known for delivering first-rate stories and conducting legendary interviews and responsible for raising the level of reporting and news that their respective networks are known for. They continued working until they decided to go. They weren't fired. Cronkite retired at sixty-five and Walters worked at the same network for thirty-eight years, retiring in May 2014. When a transfer in power means the new regime is unable to see how important that basic human factor is, and they begin laying people off and replacing them with young, inexperienced candidates, they're killing the company's spirit. That's what I feel happened at Univision the year my show was canceled.

Before continuing, I'd like to make one thing clear: Technically, I was not fired; I was told they had decided to discontinue my show, but they wanted to keep me in the network for specials. And the decision didn't come from Univision the network, but rather, from the president at the time, someone who barely even knew me, and who in the end lasted only a few years in that position. But put yourself in my shoes: When you have a weekly show with high ratings and are told that it's going to be canceled and replaced by a couple of one-time specials, don't you think that's an offer that leaves a lot to be desired? It's the classic corporate move where they don't "fire" you, but rather offer you something they know you'll be unwilling to accept because you're not interested or because it has nothing to do with what you've been doing for so many years. It's just another way of firing you, but without written evidence. That's why, many times, when I speak of this moment in my life, I can't help but use the word "fired," because that's what I felt. And let me tell you, it was one of the most traumatic events of my life. But, before I get into how I felt and how I decided to not give up, let me start at the beginning.

Contrary to most industries, the longer television contracts last, the worse they are. When you sign a TV contract, you do so for a fixed amount of money. With time, if you improve and make more money for the network, you are still locked in to the fixed amount stipulated in your contract until it expires. This means you can get stuck earning the same salary for six years straight. It's not advisable and less than ideal. So, one day, I approached Ray Rodríguez, president of Univision at the time, and said, "Look, how about if we do this. Since you and I argue so much, let's renegotiate my contract once a year. If, after the year is over, you aren't unhappy with me and I'm not unhappy with you, I'll sign it again." And that's what we did for eight or nine years straight. Yes, we fought, but in the end we also reached an agreement. There was an implicit mutual respect between us.

In 2009, Ray was training his successor while he prepared to retire from the network, which happened at the end of that year. Just like with the change of power at the White House, the day Ray retired, part of his team left with him. A young man of thirty-five was named Univision Network's new president, and that's when they began draining employees out of the company.

They fired people with years of experience and replaced them with new, young, and, in some cases, inexperienced people. It was clear to me that they were attempting to remove the older employees and replace them with younger people; they were hoping to radically change the network, and while doing so they created a disaster.

Some weeks, they laid off dozens of people in a single day, many of whom had worked there practically their entire lives. The layoffs that began at the end of 2009 broke our hearts because, up until then, everyone who worked at Univision had been like a great big family.

To be totally honest, I thought I would be immune to these changes. Actually, many of the people who surrounded us thought the same thing. It never crossed anyone's mind that Marcos and I would be directly affected by the tornado hitting

Univision because my show had lasted twenty-one years on the air and we were still making a lot of money for the network. At the time, one of the most recent shows to air was one where I had interviewed the multitalented Mexican artist Lucero; the show had received a nineteen-point bump in ratings and was a huge success. There was no reason to worry, or at least that's what we thought the day we were called into the network offices for a meeting.

I can't recall vivid details like what I was wearing that day, but I do remember asking Marcos what this guy wanted with us, since we barely knew him. But Marcos said, "He probably wants to meet us in person and talk about renegotiating the contract." So, off we went to the office, absolutely clueless about what was coming. We arrived, sat down in the waiting room, and, as usual, I began to chitchat with the assistant, who had been the former president's assistant. As we spoke, I noticed she was fidgety and nervous. Now I realize she probably already knew the hammer was about to fall, and she didn't really know what to say under the circumstances.

They finally asked us into the office. We were greeted by two of the new main executives at the network's helm. They asked me where I wanted to sit and I chose the seat I always took when I negotiated with Ray. As we began to talk, I felt thick tension in the air. After some small talk, we began discussing our contract negotiation, the reason Marcos and I assumed we had been called to this meeting, but suddenly the conversation took a strange turn. Their nerves were on edge and we couldn't figure out what they were trying to tell us. Finally, the executives revealed the true reason for this meeting: They had decided to cancel *The Cristina Show.* They went on to explain that they thought the timing was ideal because the show was still successful and this would give us the chance to end it on a high note.

This news took us completely by surprise and hit us like a ton of bricks. We didn't know how to react. Then suddenly, Marcos turned to one of the executives and said, "Hang on, have you seen the ratings we had last Monday?" Of course they had, yet they insisted this decision wasn't based on ratings. We were stunned. With that response, Marcos jumped out of his seat, looked at me, and said, "Let's go, come on." I asked him to wait, turned to the man who had been speaking, and asked, furiously, "Are you firing me?" To which they all immediately responded not at all, that this was my home, that they had other plans for me, that they wanted me to stay and do some specials for the network.

We just couldn't believe our ears. Those specials they kept mentioning were actually just two one-off shows. In other words, I was to go from having a weekly show to two shows and that was it. It was obvious what those "specials" really entailed. They wanted me to sign a contract for these two specials so they could make sure I couldn't work with anyone else for a while; that is, they basically wanted to keep me off the market, lock me up and throw away the key. It was incredibly strange, dare I say even personal. It made no sense. The ratings were very high, they had said so themselves. Their reasoning poured over us like a bucket of ice water.

Since the new executives in power wanted to change the network, aside from laying off so many people, they also began changing the network's look as well as its shows. They began remodeling the sets to modernize them, which wasn't well received because our audience felt it looked a bit cold. One of the basic problems they had with us, given this general change in image they were after, was that our contract gave us total creative control of our show, and that was a major disadvantage to them. What began to happen was that if they didn't like something we had done on the show, they would call to tell us we had to edit it out. However, by contract, they had no right to demand we take anything out, even if what we were doing could affect some other business they might be negotiating.

Actually, this type of back and forth had always gone on. When we began working at Univision, we also had to put up a fight, because we were breaking the mold and defending what we believed in. It was always like that; however, it used to be a much more cordial battle. There was a dialogue. The previous president didn't demand that we take something out of our show; he would call and explain the conflict of interest so that we could work together to find a solution that satisfied all parties. We helped each other out. With the new team, however, it became an all-out war. When the new executives, managers, and directors came on the scene, they tried to command respect by imposing their ideas and changes without taking the time to understand the history of each of us at the network, the battles won and lost, the struggles . . . everything that ultimately went into making an organization like Univision.

As we stood up to leave they asked when I would get back to them regarding the specials, and I politely asked for some time to think about it. When we left the building, Marcos and I got into our car and drove straight to our local neighborhood bar.

We sat at a table and Marcos ordered a double whiskey and I asked for a martini. We couldn't believe what had just happened. We stared at each other, our thoughts rapidly firing the same questions: *What went on in there? What was that? They just robbed and killed us for no apparent reason.* In that instant, I wasn't angry. What I felt in that moment was pure shock. I just couldn't understand it. It wasn't until much later that the pain and depression would set in and penetrate every fiber of my being.

We made them wait a couple of months for our response, although we already knew it would be no. Meanwhile, I went from absolute shock to sheer indignation. Our contract was valid through the end of the year and they broke the news to us in August, so we still had a few months of work ahead of us.

Another thing that happened that same day they told us they were going to cancel *The Cristina Show* was that they prohibited us from breaking the news to our employees, who, as a result of the show's cancellation, would be left jobless. The executives explained that they were going to talk to them first, but we said no. We wanted to tell our employees first and then they could come in later to deliver the details of the layoff. They insisted on being present, at the very least, when we gave our employees the news, but we remained firm and once again said no. Marcos and I wanted to talk to our people first so they'd have enough time to digest this sudden change in all of our lives. Besides, I didn't want these executives to swoop in and say that the show was ending for reasons other than the truth. I wanted to make sure our employees heard the real story from me; it was the least I could do after so many years of loyalty and hard work.

Since we owned the studio where we filmed the show, we were in control of the situation, and the executives finally had to accept our conditions.

When we finally delivered the news to our people, they were as stunned as we had been. Many of them had been working on the show since the beginning. Some broke down in tears, while others were simply speechless. It was an extremely difficult moment for all of us, not only due to the surprise and confusion caused by finding out you no longer have a job, but also because our work team functioned as a close family. Therefore, the decision not only had individual repercussions, it affected us as a family. We immediately joined forces and Marcos and I did all we could to find new jobs for our team so that they wouldn't be left out on the street. It was an incredibly sad process for us all.

Meanwhile, Marcos spoke to the executives again to finish programming what was left of the show, but all they asked us to do was record one last episode, the final good-bye. They weren't interested in any other programs, just that one. The feeling we got was that the sooner we were done, the better. I felt they wanted to destroy us, to use us as an example for anyone else who desired to be independent within the company. But they weren't successful, because I never give up.

At first, they asked us to do a two-hour finale, which would benefit the advertising companies and distract our viewers from what was really going on, but we managed to negotiate it down to one hour. They wanted us to announce that I was retiring, but I refused because that wasn't the case; taking *The Cristina Show* off the air wasn't by choice.

While all of this went down, Marcos finally gave them our

answer to their "specials" offer: "No, we do not accept it." They were extremely bothered by this reply. I think they didn't expect me to say no because in such big and powerful companies, those below the executives usually never win because they supposedly have no say in the situation. But that wasn't true in my case. They sent lawyers to continue negotiations, to scare us a bit, but our minds were made up. It's the perfect example of how, in order to successfully negotiate, you must know what you're worth and be willing to leave it all, a concept we'll explore later in chapter 10. I knew all too well what I was worth, and I didn't deserve to be treated this way, so I had to leave.

> *To successfully negotiate, you must know what you're worth and be willing to leave it all.*

The last show had big artists, such as Joan Sebastian, Fernando Colunga, and Gloria Estefan, among others, but the person who best expressed herself on the program was my daughter Titi. "After having my mom do this for so many years, the love you all have for her can be felt throughout the whole family. Thank you," she said through her tears. For me, it was the most heart-wrenching moment in the entire show. I still get emotional thinking about her words and remembering this sudden awful event that not only affected me, but impacted my whole family as well. Toward the end of that final hour, after thanking everyone who had made the show possible as well as the loyal audience and fans who had supported me for twenty-one years, I looked straight into the camera and firmly said, "I'm not retiring. There's still enough Cristina to go around for a long time . . . a long time . . . a long time." No one was going to push me aside and make everyone believe I was retiring, hell no! Not even while experiencing the most unexpected and painful moment in my career did I ever think about giving up.

After we filmed that show, we threw an amazing party at the studio, with celebrity guests and the whole nine yards. But truthfully, in that instant I felt absolutely numb. My emotions were completely paralyzed by the shock, and in my mind, I had already left the building.

Knowledge Is Power

Losing a job overnight is an extremely traumatic moment. Here are some tips for dealing with this emotional situation in the best way possible:

1. Remain calm at work. That's not the place to vent your anger and frustration.
2. It's okay if you need a moment to mourn after such a shock. Take time to heal and think about what the best next step should be to continue your journey.
3. Don't lose hope and don't give up.

To finalize our exit, Marcos had to return to the network to negotiate the last details before we closed this chapter in our lives. It was like a divorce: We had to figure out what to do with our studio—which they rented for other shows—with our employees, and with every other aspect entailed in ending a twenty-one-year relationship. They had forbidden me to go to press with my story. So, while enduring such confusion and pain, I had an additional frustration: When I went to Kmart to promote Casa Cristina, our home decor line, for instance, the people waiting in line for my autograph would ask, "Cristina, why did you abandon us?" when they reached me. I'm no one without my fans, and seeing the pain on their faces and feeling their sense of abandonment broke my heart. I longed with every ounce of my being to give them a straight answer and tell them I hadn't abandoned them, but I couldn't utter a word! Yet they continued asking, one after the other, until I finally broke protocol and said, "I didn't leave. I was fired." What ensued next was an endless war of words where the Univision executives refuted what I said and vice versa.

They were driving me crazy and, eventually, all of that back and forth, together with the trauma I had just experienced, pushed me to my limit. That December, when I was finally on vacation at home, I succumbed to a deep depression. I watched as the power changed hands and the new team in command pulled apart a network we had all built together with years of hard work and sacrifices. Univision wasn't even half of what it had been before . . . and not surprisingly, today most of the people who were in power during this fateful time are no longer there.

The deepest pain I felt came from the fact that, through the years, I had always felt like I belonged to the Univision family. When that new group of executives slammed the door in my face overnight, it felt like my family was abandoning me; it felt like I no longer even had a family, and as a result, I plunged into a profound depression.

Losing my job was like a jab to my gut, but losing my family was heart-wrenching. After sharing twenty-one years, the loneliness I felt brought on by no longer being around my employees and colleagues, by seeing them unemployed, and by knowing we were all suddenly completely spread out around Miami and no longer together, left me feeling devastated and helpless.

No one likes change. I wanted my work family to remain intact, but that was out of my hands. Life is a series of changes and decisions, giving us experiences from which we must learn and grow. It wasn't easy, but gradually I was able to move forward after ending my career at Univision and discover that every cloud has a silver lining. And, although I didn't know it yet, I would soon learn that we must all be flexible and keep our eyes open. By noticing what's going on around us, we can make clear decisions about our next destinations—and continue learning from every step we take along the way.

No matter how painful and difficult the changes in your life may seem, whenever you feel like giving up, don't. Instead, rise up and shine! If you pick yourself up and keep moving forward, you will be able to see that the light shining at the end of the tunnel might be coming from a new door that is within your reach, ready for you to step through and start a new chapter in your life. Go, open that door, and continue your journey.

> *Life is a series of changes and decisions, giving us experiences from which we must learn and grow.*

PUT IT TO WORK IN YOUR LIFE!

1. Never give up. If you fall, dust yourself off, rise up, and shine.
2. Even if you are at the top of your game, at the height of your career, by no means does that mean you are no longer swimming with the sharks.
3. Remain aware of what's going on around you.
4. When the time comes to negotiate, you must know your worth and be willing to leave.
5. Change is difficult, but absolutely necessary. That is how you will learn the greatest lessons of your life.

9

Embrace Your Ambition

When associated with a woman, "ambition" still sounds like a dirty word, but if we use it to describe a man, it's what we expect a man to be if he's striving to be successful in life. Let's put it into context. If you hear someone say that a man is "ambitious," what do you think? The first thing that probably crosses your mind is that he knows what he wants and will go far because he can clearly see the path he must take to be successful. Now, let's try again: What do you think or feel when you're told that a certain woman is ambitious? Let's be honest. Many of you probably had a flash image of a lioness eating whoever gets in her way as she does everything in her power to reach her goals. Because ambition has such a negative connotation for women even today, many of us steer clear of this adjective. How can a single word provoke such different connotations when used to describe a man or a woman? Don't you think it should mean the same thing, regardless of the person's gender? After all, aren't we all just human beings?

Society and our families have instilled in us a reflex that makes us instantly feel that "an ambitious woman" isn't necessarily a good thing. That's why many powerful women, when asked if they're ambitious, do whatever possible to avoid that specific word and redefine that desire for success that springs from deep within by using different words. Let's not fool ourselves. That feeling, that burning desire to be successful at what you do, is purely and exclusively called *ambition*, and there's nothing wrong with it!

Professional ambition does not kill a man or woman. It actually serves as motivation to go after what we want, to accomplish our dreams. You mustn't run away from this term; accept it and feel proud that today you are a woman who has the right to be ambitious and follow the open roads ahead of you to achieve whatever you set your mind to. We must celebrate ambitious women instead of punishing them.

I had the chance to see my best friends, Gloria and Emilio Estefan, make it big. When I met them, they were just starting out and lived in a modest house with very little money. I saw what happened to them, how all of their hard work paid off and they became extremely successful, and I supported and was happy for them. And finally, one day I turned to Marcos and said, "You know what? Now it's my turn." Gloria and Emilio inspired me, and instead of watching from the sidelines or looking over my shoulder to see what was behind me, I began focusing on what lay ahead.

> *We must celebrate ambitious women instead of punishing them.*

My Name Is Cristina Saralegui and I Am an Ambitious Woman

I don't have a problem saying I'm ambitious. I know that without my ambition, I wouldn't be where I am today. I actually figured out early on that it wasn't a bad thing to be an ambitious woman, even though oftentimes, society, along with our families, tries to make us believe the contrary.

Knowledge Is Power

According to a 2012 Pew Research Center survey, sixty-six percent of women between the ages of eighteen and thirty-four say that having a well-paid job is "one of the most important things" or "very important" in their lives, compared to fifty-nine percent of men.

I had bold and beautiful ambitions as a young woman. I wanted to have a big life—really big—traveling and seeing the world, learning, and changing people's lives. I believe these desires and ambitions come from my father and grandfather, who were my inspiration. They were entrepreneurs and doers who accomplished whatever they set their minds to. I knew that's what I wanted for myself. However, having a Basque background made the road tougher, because if you're a woman in a Basque family, it's like you don't even exist. You're invisible. That word, that feeling, tormented me. It's not that I necessarily wanted to be important or famous back then; what I truly desired—my ambition—was to stop being *invisible*. And I felt that invisibility due to being a woman right down to the smallest detail. For example, every man in my family is named Francisco—one of my brothers, Patxi (which means Francisco in Basque); his son, Frankie; my father, Francisco; my grandfather, Francisco—but I wasn't able to be part of that tradition because I was a girl. And that made me feel . . . invisible.

But I didn't let that invisibility control me. Absolutely not. I had to fight long and hard to be heard within my family, to receive their support. When I began my first TV show, an uncle had nothing better to say than, "The audacity of ignorance." No one supported me, so I had to support myself. But I didn't let that bring me down; my ambition was stronger than anything else, and that's how I managed to reach my dreams and live the life I had always wanted. I then met the person with whom I was able to share this bold dream: Marcos became the person who supported me unconditionally in everything and against all odds—and his ambitions include being ambitious on my behalf. So, why should I have to hide the fact that I'm an ambitious person? On the contrary, I not only don't want to hide it, I want to celebrate it. And I want you to have the courage to do the same. Embrace your ambition, there's absolutely nothing wrong with it.

The Power of Ambition

Ambition is a positive trait. There's no reason for you to have modest goals, quite the opposite: Don't be afraid to express how far you want to get in life. In other words, don't be afraid to show your ambitious side. And if someone asks if you have ambitions or if you consider yourself an ambitious woman, don't respond with the modest phrases people expect to hear. You must learn how to speak with authority and confidence. Be firm and focus on your goals. Note: Being strong and having power is not a bad thing. In my eyes, the definition of power is being able to do what you please with your life. Careful, this definitely doesn't imply that you can do what you please with other people's lives; it's about doing what you want with *your life*. We, both men and women, are allowed to do whatever we want with our lives, and no one should make you believe otherwise.

I've applied this principle in my own life by always making sure to have creative control of my TV show, my magazines, and whatever else crosses my career path. I often tell my daughter Titi, who's a banker, that if something isn't working, she has to learn how to *"darle la vuelta."* This is a very Cuban phrase that means turning it around to get your way, finding a creative solution to the problem without making enemies, and it's a great piece of advice. I wasn't interested in having a boss tell me what I had to write about for the magazine. When they sent me to interview someone or to cover a story I didn't find interesting, after a while, I learned how to *darle la vuelta* and do it my way, without causing any friction or problems with my boss.

> *The definition of power is being able to do what you please with your life.*

Today, women have the opportunity to do whatever they want because of the women before them who paved the way and opened doors so it would be okay to desire a career. If this hadn't happened, we would still all be at home, cooking over a hot stove, even if we hated the kitchen. What I want is for all women

Knowledge Is Power

The sixties changed the course of history for women in the United States. That decade gave way to the renowned sexual revolution, more women than ever entering the workforce, movements seeking equal pay beginning to emerge, and the birth control pill becoming available, allowing eighty percent of women within reproductive ages to go on the pill to avoid unwanted pregnancies, and therefore have more freedom to do what they wanted with their lives.

to apply themselves and aim for higher ambitions, including those whose skills mainly lie in the home and kitchen. For example, if you love to cook and entertain, look into starting your own catering business. Or if you bake amazing cakes, focus your ambition on selling your cakes in every supermarket in the United States, earning good money and maybe even becoming famous.

If you discover you're great at one particular thing, that's where your ambition comes into play. Being the best at what you do is essential to a successful life. Take Edda, for example, a friend of mine who makes fabulous cakes. When Hurricane Andrew hit Miami and left the city without electricity, Edda came up with an idea to save her cakes from spoiling: She sliced them,

Being the best at what you do is essential to a successful life.

put them in her gas oven, and toasted the pieces. In this way, her unique and delicious biscotti-like treats were born, which she later sold and turned into an incredibly successful business. And she did all that in the middle of a hurricane! As mentioned in chapter 2, you never know when a new passion or vocation will present itself. You must keep your eyes peeled and remain aware of your surroundings. Then, when you see the right opportunity, take action, apply your ambition to that new calling, and take it as far as you can possibly go.

Redefining Ambition for Women

To turn your passion into a successful career, to bury the negative connotation of the word "ambition" when it's associated with women, I want you to continue applying its true meaning in your life: to no longer be invisible, to be financially independent, and to do whatever you want rather than what others want you to do. Ambition is a positive quality; it reflects the dreams you want to accomplish; it means that you want to be successful and desire acknowledgment for all you do. Don't be afraid to be ambitious and express it. You deserve whatever you want.

Here are a few ways to start:

1. Demystify the word "ambition"—it's not negative, it's positive.
2. Forget about what other people will say. It doesn't matter what others think or say; focus instead on what you want to accomplish with your ambition.
3. Make this word, this trait, work in your favor: With ambition you can achieve your biggest goals.

The biggest professional challenge I ever had to face was television. When I entered into the world of TV, I'd never worked in this medium before. I didn't know what to expect and I learned the hard way. The pilot for *The Cristina Show*, the first episode we taped, was done in a church's dining hall. I'm very shy and I remember being so scared that, when they gave me the microphone, my hands were drenched in sweat. Throughout the taping, the hand I used to hold the mike was perspiring so profusely that I worried about getting electrocuted. (I used to have major panic attacks, so much so that I owe the first few years of *The Cristina Show* to Xanax.) But I wasn't going to let fear win, because fear is useless. And what made me charge forward through my panic and fear was my ambition, the desire for success.

Men aren't worried about being called ambitious; it's actually a compliment. And it should be one for women, too. Don't be ashamed or embarrassed to express that you, too, want to succeed in what you do. Ambition pushes you to be the best you can be, and that, in turn, helps you reach your goals and dreams. So, why not celebrate this desire to succeed instead of hiding it for fear of being judged?

When people say that women aren't as ambitious as men, that's a lie. Do you mean to tell me a woman in politics doesn't want to achieve the same goals as male politicians, or that a female musician doesn't want the same fame and recognition as her male counterparts? Well, that's ambition! There's that word again, present in all we do. And it has been around for centuries. Take, for example, Hatshepsut, the queen of Egypt who managed to become pharaoh. Granddaughter, daughter, and wife of pharaohs, her ambition and pride made her reclaim the throne that was rightfully hers. Being queen was not enough for her; her goal, her ambition, was to become pharaoh. And she did. She governed as pharaoh for twenty-two years, holding the throne longer than any other woman in Egypt's history. Without ambition, she wouldn't have made history the way she did.

However, to govern, Hatshepsut decided to wear the pharaoh's beard. In other words, she felt the need to appear "macho" to occupy such a position. Today, fortunately, she wouldn't need to do this. Yet, through the years, I've seen many women act similarly. They've completely lost their femininity. That's no longer necessary. And this is a key point for women who are reclaiming and redefining ambition as it relates to their own lives. I've said that being ambitious is good, and that both men and women have the same right to be ambitious and be seen as equals, but that doesn't mean you have to dress or look the same. You don't have to wear a suit and tie or stop using makeup to be taken seriously. You must continue being true to yourself. The key to success lies in your self-esteem, not your clothes. To be successful you must have self-confidence and know what you're worth (see chapter 10). We all have the right to be ambitious and fight for what we want.

Solidarity Trumps Envy

Solidarity is essential if we're going to smash the stereotype that being an ambitious woman is not a positive thing. If we all join forces and help each other, men and women alike, if we support one another, if we set aside all envy and celebrate other women's accomplishments, this will help us demolish the myth that ambition is bad when describing a woman and her goals. Unfortunately, this solidarity, this support among women, is still very weak.

Ambition doesn't have to trump solidarity and generosity.

This is up to you and how you decide to handle your success. Being ambitious doesn't mean leaving your colleagues, friends, and family behind. On the contrary, you must be supportive of those around you to truly lead a successful life.

A few years back, when we had gone to Chicago to tape *The Cristina Show*, we wanted to rent Oprah Winfrey's studio, but realized we needed more space. When we took the show on the road, thousands of people came to see us. In any case, Oprah was very generous. While we were there, I went to one of her tapings and Oprah told her audience, "This woman has been called the Latina Oprah, but that's not true. I'm the black Cristina." I almost peed in my chair. That's a clear example of the solidarity that should exist between women in both our professional and personal worlds. You must learn to be generous with your knowledge, your contacts, and whatever else you have to give.

One of the things that bothers me most about some of the men I know in business is that they won't give you even one contact to help you out. This has also happened with many journalists I've met throughout my career. A journalist will lend you his typewriter, but never his contacts, and God forbid he calls someone on your behalf. I will. And you know why? Because generosity is the key to a long-lasting career. Every person I've helped throughout my career, whom I've put in important positions, continues to come back. It's karma: Everything you throw out into the universe will come back to you, both the good energy and the bad.

> *Generosity is the key to a long-lasting career.*

At the same time, you can't let people walk all over you. You must be able to detect those who are good-for-nothings, who suck the life out of you, who adhere to you like leeches and consume your energy with their envy. They not only want what you have, they also don't want you to have it. I never understood this. There's enough to go around for everyone! Yes, we all feel envy at some point in our lives, but you have to banish it immediately. As I've said before in this book, envy is the cancer of the soul; we must cut it out of our lives and never let it show up again. It's the most negative feeling we can experience and, as such, we must reject it and never let it emerge again. Once you've gotten rid of this feeling, look around and support your colleagues.

Solidarity among professional women is almost nonexistent and that's a problem. While editor in chief at *Cosmopolitan en Español*, I was also in charge of twenty-six special publications for the company, for which I was paid separately. It represented one-third of my salary. When I returned from my maternity leave after giving birth to Jon Marcos, I had only six of those twenty-six projects left, because another editor, a colleague and so-called friend, had taken the rest. Talk about a lack of support!

Men do support each other. They're friends, they all play golf with the boss. But women don't trust and support each other nearly enough.

Throughout my career, I've felt solidarity and support from very few female colleagues, and I've seen how essential it is for us to join forces instead of each of us traveling our own paths alone. My colleague, journalist and host María Celeste Arrarás, knows what solidarity is all about. She's not afraid to roll up her

SHARING THE TRUTH

Our mothers and grandmothers not only celebrated the right of men to act like kings at home, they also raised their daughters to think that other women will steal our boyfriends or sleep with our husbands. You don't believe me? Think about it. When there's a woman who has just gotten a divorce, many avoid her. No one wants to be with her because now that she's single, she poses a threat. We learn from childhood not to trust other women, and that kills all possibility of solidarity later in life. We must change this by raising our daughters differently, teaching them to value and cherish their fellow women—friends and colleagues.

sleeves and get her hands dirty when it's time to work: She managed to become executive producer of her show and did it all, even personally calling guests to invite them to the show, a task usually carried out by other producers. Aside from her work ethic, she's one of the few people who was always straightforward and truthful with me. She was the first person to interview me when I moved to another network and the only one to warn me that getting celebrities to appear on my new show on Telemundo would be an uphill battle, which she knew from firsthand experience. She has been there for me ever since I met her and throughout all the time we've shared in Univision and Telemundo. I will be forever grateful to her for that.

María Celeste is an amazing example, but having said that, she shouldn't be the exception to the rule. Examples like hers should abound, and it's all up to you: Stop being so defensive.

Trust and help each other out. Don't feed into the idea that ambition is a negative quality in yourself or in any other woman, and don't forget about those around you while pursuing your goals. Be supportive and surround yourself with a good team of people. If you take these steps, you'll achieve more success than you ever imagined possible.

Don't Let Ambition Blind You

I recommend that you find a good group of colleagues at work as well as mentors and people who support you in other aspects of your life if you want to get ahead. And, as much as you should be aware of opportunities that come knocking at your door, it's also paramount to pay attention to the advice these important people impart, because they want the best for you. Don't let ambition blind you. It's important that you trust and be supportive with others, and it's just as important for you to listen to what they have to say.

On the other hand, if someone tells me I should do something but I don't want to do it, then I don't. I'm not afraid of saying no. You must learn how to say no to avoid having people take undue advantage of you. Most of the time, when I receive suggestions, my first answer is "No." But I also remain open enough that, if I consider the advice I'm getting and it makes sense, if the points I'm presented with are valid, I'll think about it and may change my mind. In the end, if I see that the advice was on target and it's worth giving a try, I'll take it.

It's important to learn how to say no, but it's equally important to learn how to listen. If you allow yourself to listen to

> *It's important to learn how to say no, but it's equally important to learn how to listen.*

what other trusted people on your team have to say, that opens up discussions that could lead to good ideas. Some will be carried out, others won't, but it's key to respect each person's different opinion. Knowing how to listen and learn from what another person may be able to offer you—a new perspective, his or her experiences—combined with your own ambition, can help you get ahead in your career and life. Don't throw these opportunities away.

The Evolution of Ambition in Your Life

Ambitions come in all different sizes. It's up to you to figure out the size and type of ambition you have. This can change as you mature. Many women want to be able to do it all. Fine. They want to have the perfect house, cook better than anyone in their neighborhoods, clean and leave everything spotless, raise perfect children, and, on top of all that, have careers. Well, they're in for a surprise! Here's another secret to success: You can do it all, but not all at the same time. We'll dive into this concept in chapter 14, but for now I want to emphasize that you can't realistically cling to the ambition of being the best at everything at the same time. That's why ambitions come in different sizes and each one has its ideal time and place.

Today, many professionals set disproportionate demands on themselves, especially with regard to age. Some ask themselves, "I'm thirty years old. What have I done in these thirty years when compared to my colleagues or to the people I admire?" Damn, Alexander the Great died at thirty-two, but those were other times. Don't do that to yourself. Don't compare your age to what you've accomplished, because it's not about that. Each person has his or her own personal journey. Some will accomplish things at a young age, while others will reach

> *You can do it all, but not all at the same time.*

their dreams as they mature. The key is to stay focused on what you want and continue traveling toward your goals no matter what age you are.

Young people sometimes have blind ambition driving them forward, but with time, it's important to stop and think about what you really want, where you see yourself in the future, what would make you truly happy, and adjust your goals according to the changes that come with age. For instance, today ambition and my career aren't as important to me because I've already achieved my biggest goals. So, having been such an ambitious person, life has taught me that with time, experience, and success, your ambition for some things will change or decrease, leaving you with a purpose that offers deeper meaning in your life. No matter how ambitious you are, you must never lose sight of your purpose. Ambition evolves with your changing goals, and to achieve your desires, you must first figure out where you're heading. As I discussed earlier in this book, without goals, you can't have a clear path toward making your dreams come true. If this concept is still a bit fuzzy for you, go back to chapter 3, which will help you create a map of your goals and dreams to reach your desired destination.

PUT IT TO WORK FOR YOU!

1. Remove the negative connotation from the word "ambition."
2. Learn how to openly express your ambitions and how far you want to go. Remember, you can do whatever you want with your life.
3. Try to be the best at what you do.
4. Be supportive with your colleagues, both women and men. You'll get more done if you join forces.
5. Make sure your ambition has a deeper purpose than just making money.

10

Know Your Worth and Ask for What You Deserve

N o matter what area in your life, you will encounter many situations where you'll have to negotiate for both small and large things, ranging from who's going to take the kids to soccer practice to your salary or the purchase of a home. Before you can become adept at negotiating for what you deserve, you must first know your worth.

However, even before you can assess your worth, discovering your true value will require mastering a crucial step: You must possess a high level of self-esteem and self-confidence. Without these two basic elements, even if you know your monetary worth, you'll lack the confidence to evaluate and ask for what you truly deserve.

I spent twenty years working in the magazine world and the following twenty-two in television. Before moving into television, I remember Marcos saying, "You're already too comfortable in the editorial world. Why don't you challenge yourself to do something else? Let's get into television, come on, let's do it!" And I thought he was crazy. He wanted to push me to do something different, something that would challenge me to learn something new, like write a book, do TV, or try anything that was far from the magazine business, which I could handle with my eyes closed. I accepted the challenge and jumped into television, and the rest is history. Nevertheless, one of the reasons I was able to take that risky leap was because I knew what I was worth—I had self-confidence—and although I'm no fan of change, I knew Marcos was right. I needed to challenge myself to continue growing in my career and learn new skills. Now I challenge you. Discover your worth in your professional and personal life and find the self-confidence you need to ask for what you deserve, always!

Discover Your Worth

To discover what you're worth, you must first ensure that your self-esteem and self-confidence are high. Why? Well, because if your self-confidence wavers and you lack faith in yourself, it will be much harder for you to convince others of your value, be it a company, family, or friends.

Knowledge Is Power

A Dove Self-Esteem survey revealed that seven out of ten girls believe they aren't good enough or don't measure up in certain areas, including personal appearance, school performance, and their relationships with friends and family members. This must change. We must know what we are worth to set a good example for our daughters and encourage them to have high levels of self-confidence and self-esteem.

Your Self-Esteem

If you have a low self-esteem, you will likely experience anxiety, depression, and a general sense of dissatisfaction with yourself. A low self-esteem can also affect your relationships with other people. By not valuing yourself, you will probably struggle to defend yourself against criticism or ask for what you deserve in both personal and professional situations. Your self-esteem affects every area of your life; if it's low, it can perpetuate a vicious circle. If you don't value yourself, this can cause anxiety or sadness, which can in turn affect your personal and professional relationships, which means you won't feel motivated to do your best on the job or feel your best around friends and family, and this potentially self-destructive behavior will only feed into your low self-esteem. You are the only one with the power to break this endless cycle and find a more positive path. Start with these three steps:

1. *Accept yourself.* We all have good and bad traits, but if you focus only on the bad, you will be feeding into a very negative self-image that can take over your life. Shake off that negativity, stop criticizing yourself, and concentrate on the positive. Pay attention to all of the good within you that you can share with others. Make a list of your strengths, your accomplishments, and what you admire about yourself. Focus on the good and keep in mind that your weaknesses can be worked on and improved. Everything has a solution and *no one is perfect*. Is that clear? No one—none of the human beings on this planet—is perfect.

2. *Don't compare yourself to others.* You are unique, so don't try to be like someone else. You can admire others, and someone can inspire and motivate you, but avoid all comparisons. This is your life and you must create your own path to do with it what you want.

3. *Do what you love.* If you dedicate your energy to doing what you love, you won't have time for negativity because you will be inspired and motivated to keep moving forward. Focus on your goals and work toward learning and outdoing yourself. Once you're okay with yourself, you'll see that being firmer regarding your decisions will come naturally because you'll know your worth.

Your Self-Confidence

Although self-esteem and self-confidence seem like two similar concepts, they have one key difference: Self-esteem reflects how you feel about yourself, while self-confidence is related to how you feel about your skills, and that can vary. You may have a high self-esteem, but not feel confident about your math skills. If you're starting a small business, for instance, that particular lack of self-confidence will hold you back. If deep down you know you could do the math if you tried, you need to ask yourself why you feel insecure and try to conquer that insecurity.

To begin this process, examine the root of your insecurity. Ask yourself the necessary questions to understand where these fears originated and face your insecurities. Write them down, analyze them, talk about them with your loved ones, and seek support for overcoming them. No matter what you do, don't let your lack of self-confidence paralyze you. In this case, for instance, you could sign up for a math class online or at a community college to brush up on rusty math skills and boost your confidence. Elevating both your self-esteem and self-confidence isn't easy, but it is possible. Don't give up. Just as I suggested with your self-esteem, in this case you should also write down your accomplishments, everything you know you do well, and allow yourself to feel good about the positive results. Modesty is not a welcome guest at this party. Think about your skills and what you're good at. This will help you discover what you're worth. If you're the only one who can do a specific task at home or at the office, that has a unique value that the person standing next to you might lack. Take advantage of that competitive edge!

Once you feel more secure, another big secret to success lies in always being yourself. Be authentic. If you become someone else's product, if you let yourself be guided only by the desire for fame and wanting to have it all, you will get lost along the way, and whatever you accomplish will likely not make you happy. You must be true to yourself.

The reason you need self-confidence is to ask for what you deserve and not doubt yourself when the time comes to make important decisions. My employees both respected me and were terrified of me. Once, my executive producer, who is still a dear friend, said to me, "You can't be like that; you have to have an open-door policy. Your employees are afraid of you." And I answered, "Hey, I work real hard to make sure

If you don't believe in yourself, others won't either.

they fear me. Because I don't want them to love me, I want them to respect me."

Respect is one of the key factors to success in any type of work, and in journalism that respect comes from credibility. The day you lose your credibility, you are no one. This can actually be applied to all careers: If you lose your credibility, you risk losing the respect of others and your worth diminishes. However, in order to build credibility, apart from being an honest and responsible person, you must also possess self-confidence. If you don't believe in yourself, others won't either. Once I had confidence in myself, it led others to respect me as well. Self-confidence is essential. There will be thousands of people who will question you throughout your life, and although it's important to maintain an open mind and be able to admit when you are wrong, it's equally important to have enough self-confidence to support your actions and not have to explain yourself.

When we started Casa Cristina, each time we signed a new contract to design furniture, towels, or sheets I had to meet with the executives to explain who we are as Latinos. I had to school them. The last time this happened was with President Obama's campaign. That's when I realized how little many people know about the differences between a Mexican, Chilean, Guatemalan, or Dominican person. I had to explain why we are the way we are and what we like. Many executives still didn't quite get what motivates our different communities. On both occasions, as well as in many others, I had to explain our worth as Hispanics who are made up of many different peoples. Therefore, you mustn't only know what you're worth as an individual, but also as a member of a particular community, whatever your cultural or ethnic background.

Ask for What You Deserve

Conquer your fears and ask for what you deserve not only on the job, but also in life. I'm willing to give in, but I have limits, and those are the things that define my values. You have to speak up in life and say who you are and ask for what you want. The squeaky wheel gets the grease.

SHARING THE TRUTH

If you know your worth, you'll be able to recognize if you're in a relationship with someone who appreciates you, and if you aren't, you'll have the strength to leave that situation and negotiate a better partnership next time. If you know your worth, you'll be able to say no to situations that aren't good for you, and you'll be able to stand your ground and recognize your strengths. Knowing your worth also includes understanding your weaknesses without letting them define you. Build enough self-confidence to not only know what you bring to the table at work or in a relationship, but also to clearly see your weaknesses, so you can value yourself and use your strengths in your favor.

When we negotiated my first contract with Univision, I asked my lawyer, David Bercuson, who Marcos knew from his days with Miami Sound Machine, "What does *talent* mean?" David explained that "talent" was the person in front of the camera.

So I said, "I want to be referred to as a *journalist*." I asked him to comb through the contract and replace the word "talent" with "journalist" because I knew what I was worth. As a journalist, you can be the talent or the producer, without being boxed into one category. I quickly noticed that if you're just the talent in front of the camera, everyone talks about you, in front of you, as if you aren't there. "Make her stand to the side." "Do this to her." "Fix her hair or cover up her wrinkles." The real you is invisible. I knew I wasn't just the talent; I was so much more. So I asked Univision's president at the time, Joaquín Blaya, "What does an executive producer do?" When he explained it was like being the boss, I said, "Well, then I'm the executive producer." I was coming from a magazine where I managed several departments and I wasn't willing to become anyone's puppet.

Another strange thing that happened while negotiating that first contract was that I was told I had to lose my Cuban accent. I adamantly said no—Julio Iglesias has a Spanish accent, Don Francisco a Chilean one, Mexicans speak with their Mexican accent. Yet they argued that people associated tropical accents with a lack of education. So I replied, "Well, they'll just have to get used to it, because I'm not changing it. And if landing this job is dependent on me getting rid of my Cuban accent, then I don't want it." Never lose sight of who you are. You must be self-confident in order to stand your ground in situations that might compromise your integrity and to ask for what you deserve.

> *Never lose sight of who you are.*

How to Ask for a Raise

One of the most frequently asked questions Marcos and I get is from women wondering how to request a raise. They feel insecure and don't know where to begin. The main problem is that, as women, we tend to ask for a raise by explaining why we need it—"I just had a baby." "My husband lost his job."— instead of stating why we deserve it.

You must ask for a raise based on your merits, not on your needs and emotions. And to do this, you must know your worth. Most women don't know how much they contribute to their companies. Find out what your arduous work yields for your place of employment. Research the company and find a way to get the information you need to figure out how much you're worth within that place, so you can ask for what you deserve. It's also important to find out what sort of salary your male colleagues at work are commanding and compare your salary with theirs.

Both in my magazine and television careers, I've often found myself in situations where my bosses have said that my magazine isn't circulating or my show doesn't have good ratings, yet having done my homework, I knew how my job performance affected the company positively, so I could refute those arguments with concrete numbers. Staying informed is an incredible tool when it comes to negotiating and commanding respect.

But it's not just about numbers. Aside from researching the market and figuring out how much you contribute to the company monetarily, it's also important to know what makes you stand out from the crowd. What qualities make you special to this company? Is this job something you could do somewhere else? If this is the case, would another company pay you more? When asking for a raise, you must know what your contributions are worth to the company, so you can negotiate in your favor.

The other big secret when it comes to asking for a raise or negotiating a new contract is that you have to be willing to walk away and leave it all. Many of the Univision journalists sought out Marcos for advice on how to negotiate their contracts. Once, Marcos said to one of them, "Well, if they don't give you what you want, you have to be willing to leave, so tell them that." When she heard this, she was completely taken aback. "How could I say such a thing?" she asked in shock. She didn't do it. She's still a journalist, but if she's not willing to take that chance, she'll never get the salary she deserves.

If you're not committed to walking away from a deal when a negotiation doesn't satisfy your expected outcome you'll never have the power to stand firm on what you think you deserve. Additionally, negotiating on the basis of your merits and your willingness to leave shows that you place an appropriate value on your own worth, which will make the company respect and appreciate you more.

> *You have to be willing to leave.*

When I first started my career in television, I was assigned to an executive producer who wasn't granting me the creative control I had negotiated for in my contract. One day, while I was meeting with the show's advertisers in New York, that man called Univision's lawyer and told her he was the executive producer of my show and was working on the budget, so he needed to know how much I made to add it to his calculations. The lawyer told him, and he almost had a heart attack because it was thirty times more than what he made. When I found out, I called my friend Joaquín Blaya, Univision's president, and said, "You know what? I'm not taping. So you'll have to deal with all these advertisers, because I'm not going to do the show." I explained all of the issues I was having with this executive producer. I didn't know why he was being so disrespectful since we hardly knew each other. And I said, "I didn't leave a job I loved after twenty years, one where I was super comfortable, to come fight with useless people." I was willing to walk away. Finally the three of us met at my request and we cleared the air.

You have to know who you are and what you want to succeed in life. I'm a journalist, as well as an awesome mother and grandmother. I may not be a domestic goddess, but that has nothing to do with me being a good and very capable woman. Today, I know I represent women well. And I've been able to reach this conclusion

> *You have to know who you are and what you want to succeed in life.*

by learning from all the pitfalls along the way. Have the self-confidence to ask for what's duly yours, not because you need it, but because you deserve it!

Stay Informed and at the Top of Your Game

You should know your worth 24-7, and to do so you must stay informed and at the top of your game in your industry. Frequently review your company's numbers, know what you contribute, and be prepared to explain your worth on the spot. If you're informed, up to date, and prepared, you've won half the battle.

You never know what the future has in store for you, believe me. You could lose your job overnight. You could be offered a new position or another job with a smaller salary than what you deserve, and if you don't know what you're worth or what someone in your position earns at other companies, your negotiating power will slip out the window. Plus, you could lose the opportunity of a lifetime. And as women, although we're closer to being paid as much as men for doing the same jobs, we're still not there yet, especially at the top of the pay scale. It's up to us to keep pushing to change that.

Knowledge Is Power

The United States Census Bureau stated that in 2012 women earned 77 cents for every dollar a man earned. Among certain groups, like Hispanics, the gap is even wider. Hispanic women earn 58 cents for every dollar earned by a Hispanic man. Don't become one of these statistics. Stay informed so you can ask for what you deserve. Let's join forces and finally make equal pay a reality.

If you have all of these tools at hand, you will not only be able to ask for what you deserve, you'll also feel more self-confident, and this will be reflected in everything you do. You're worth your weight in gold; don't let anyone ever make you doubt it.

PUT IT TO WORK FOR YOU!

1. To discover your worth, you must first build your self-esteem and self-confidence. If you don't believe in yourself, others won't either.

2. Conquer your fears and ask for what you deserve, not only at work but in life. The squeaky wheels get the grease.

3. When you ask for a raise or negotiate a new contract, do it based on your merits, not on your needs or emotions.

4. To negotiate and ask for what you deserve, you must be willing to leave.

5. Stay informed and at the top of your game in your industry and in the world around you, so you're always prepared for what the future may have in store for you.

11

Every Cloud Has a Silver Lining

In life, you will face many closed doors and many final chapters. I know these moments of big change can be hard. They are low blows and may knock you off your feet, but find the lesson in your experience and you'll soon see the way out. With hard work and persistence, you'll always be able to get back on your feet no matter what curveballs life throws your way. You just have to learn how to open the next door and continue moving forward. It's up to you to be persistent and follow my basic secrets for success: Never, never, never give up.

When my Univision show and contract ended, I fell into a deep depression. I didn't know what to do with my free time. I had worked nonstop my entire life. However, instead of staying in bed and feeling sorry for myself, I forced myself to rise and open that next door within my reach. Maybe I did it too soon. Now I know that it's healthy to take a little time to mourn such a traumatic event, but at the time, I just wanted to face the issue and find a solution. That's how the Telemundo deal came to be.

Telemundo Knocks on My Door

When the news of *The Cristina Show* being canceled and my exit from Univision went public, Telemundo immediately offered me a show on their network. The offer was a godsend for my ego, but in hindsight, I realize I shouldn't have jumped so quickly from one thing to the next. They weren't ready to produce such a huge, complicated, costly show, and I wasn't ready to start working for another company so soon after having undergone such a shock. However, we learn from everything in life, and this was yet another lesson I could absorb only through experience.

At the time, I believed that getting back to work as soon as possible might help lift my depression. So, always looking for a solution, one of my agents, Darío Brignole, spoke to Don Browne, Telemundo's president, and we came to an agreement to do a new show. At that stage of my life, I wasn't interested in doing a daily show, so I said I would accept the offer if we agreed it would be a weekly show, and so we negotiated the deal accordingly.

He kept his promise. When I signed with Don, he put my photo on every bus in Miami and other cities; the company spent a ton on national publicity; they built a gorgeous set for our show; and everything seemed to be on track. Then, out of the blue, we were hit with another shocker. After signing me to Telemundo and making the big announcement—one of his long-time dreams—Don Browne retired. I was his last hurrah before leaving. And, as in all such cases, when he left, part of his team took off with him, leaving a vacuum at the top. We had to survive yet another changing of the guards, but this time it was at a new place that we still couldn't call home. As we worked on the show's debut over the next three months, the company remained rudderless, with no president to guide it, and we were left with a two-hour show to be aired on Sundays at a time when people are out and about instead of parked in front of their TVs. However, we were already knee-deep in the project, so we didn't give up. We rose to the challenge.

Each two-hour episode took many more hours to tape because the team we'd been assigned, though always ready and willing to do the work, hadn't been trained to produce this type of show. Their lack of experience cost us a lot of time. To top things off, we came from taping a show that was a well-oiled machine, one where we were used to getting in, doing the work, and leaving efficiently and quickly. But the one at Telemundo became a clumsy and pricey act that wouldn't yield results. To produce those two weekly hours of television, we should have had twice the personnel, but since that wasn't the case, my production team worked itself into the ground. My co-executive producer and good friend, Osvaldo Oñoz, practically lived in his office.

To complicate matters, the enormous, gorgeous set they built for me didn't work well with the type of show we wanted to produce. The first day I walked into the studio, everyone was talking about the design, asking me what I thought about the decoration and the seat upholstery, but the first thing I noticed was that the set was a long rectangle rather than a square. They told me it had been built that way because now, when taping, we had to adapt to HD television requirements. The problem was that with a rectangular set, the audience wouldn't be able to see the artists' performances because that area was in a corner far removed from the people. It wasn't practical. It was beautiful, but not functional.

As if that weren't enough, we still had to face another hurdle, one of the most important ones: guest artists. The first thing some of my close friends told me when I joined Telemundo was that no one would come to our show. The rivalry between Telemundo and Univision is so powerful that there are unspoken lists of people who cannot appear on a show on one of the networks because they promoted their work on the other one first. It wasn't a new tactic and it definitely wasn't personal; this is something that has always happened. But now, we were on the other side of the fight. They tried to boycott my show on Telemundo, but since most artists were very loyal to me, they would still agree to come on when I asked them personally.

In short, everything seemed to be going wrong. No matter how much sacrifice and work we put into this new show, we just weren't able to click on any level. I would've gladly continued to invest all my time and effort if the results had been positive. But the ratings weren't what we expected, which surprised and upset me because I knew what we were worth and how much money my show could make.

So, after having recently gone through such a traumatic experience at Univision, I told Marcos that our end was near. Telemundo's new president came to my house, we held a meeting, and he finally admitted this wasn't working out. And he was right. That project wasn't working, though in retrospect I think letting it go so easily wasn't a sensible move. Just to be clear, within only one year, our endless efforts had reaped a caliber of artists that had never appeared on that network before, largely because of their loyalty to me. Yet, Marcos and I, together with our team, were upset because we felt we weren't able to move forward. We were used to working hard, investing our time, giving it our all, certain we would see results. In this case, there were no results. It was like being stuck in the mud. So, when the new executives finally said they thought it would be best to cancel the show, my reaction this time around was completely different from the one I'd had upon hearing the same news at Univision. When the Telemundo executives left my home, I was so relieved to have that obligation lifted from my shoulders that I walked into the kitchen and began singing "Born Free." I felt liberated! I was dying to leave that job. Television is a crazy world and it's a given that you'll work incredibly hard in that industry. But, when you dedicate so many hours and don't see the expected results, there's no reason to keep it going. As I've said before in this book, you must always be flexible enough in life to recognize when it's time to stop hitting your head on the wall and change direction so you can continue moving forward.

Knowledge Is Power

As Matt Monro so wisely sings in the last verse of "Born Free": "Life is worth living, but only worth living 'cause you're born free."

A Time for Reflection

With the Telemundo show cancellation, I felt a huge, ridiculous, almost giddy sense of relief. I spent the next months on Cloud Nine. When this door closed, new ones appeared. We immediately received several offers from other places, but this time we decided to take it easy and wait. All lessons come at a price. You must learn from each of them, and we had definitely learned our lesson now. The decision to jump to Telemundo was made quickly because we were hurt and in shock. We hurried things along, but the truth is that you must never make major life decisions when your emotions are running high. Stop, evaluate your situation, and review and update your goals according to the changes you have just experienced. Then, and only then, will you be ready to rise up to your next challenge.

> *Never make major life decisions when your emotions are running high.*

When I finally gave myself time to reflect on my career, I realized I was burned out on a creative level. I love television and I do want to work in it again one day. I love conducting interviews and meeting new people, but I was tired of the record labels and the deals between them and the networks that stop artists from going to whatever show they want, as well as exhausted by all of the politicking that frequently occurs among them.

That pause we finally allowed ourselves gave me the space to tell Marcos, "The next thing we do should include social issues." And so we moved ahead with my channel on Sirius XM

Radio, Cristina Radio, as well as with my radio show *Cristina Between Friends*, where I explore social issues. That's why I decided to get involved in President Obama's campaign, too. I returned to my journalistic roots to inform my audience of important issues and help improve their lives. In the process, I once again found my center and my happiness.

When one door closes, others open; however, given my experiences and personal lessons, I would also advise that, before crossing the threshold of a new door, give yourself enough time to reflect on what lies on the other side and whether that's really where you want to go. Analyze your previous steps and let yourself process what you've just experienced before you act. The decision to jump to Telemundo so quickly wasn't a well-considered action. It was a reaction; I didn't give myself time to think it through. Granting yourself time to think allows you to carefully plan your next steps and assess what's best for you. It's the ideal moment to ask yourself deeper questions, such as, "What else do I want to do with my life?" or "What would make me happy?" If there's something you always wanted to do, but never had the guts to do it, now may be the best time to give it a shot. Time gives you a new perspective on life. Take advantage of having that time if it's given to you for some reason, and use it to your advantage. Then, whenever you're ready, yes, by all means, get up, dust yourself off, and keep moving forward.

> *Time gives you a new perspective on life.*

In my case, if the Telemundo show had been a hit, I would have found myself carrying the responsibility of this program plus the sudden health issues that took over my life not long after that. Sometimes things happen when they must and, with time, we're able to see why each change came into our lives in that precise instant. If I had continued with the show, I wouldn't have paid the necessary attention to maintain my health because I had yet to learn that lesson. I would have continued stumbling and falling without knowing why; I was so focused on my career that, if the Telemundo show hadn't been canceled, I would probably be dead.

SHARING THE TRUTH

Be honest with yourself and pay attention to your needs. Don't be blinded by the emotions and reactions caused by big life changes. When I say *pa'lante*, rise up, I want to motivate you and give you energy, but I also know you need to give yourself time and space to listen to your inner voice, observe your situation from a different perspective, and reflect on the best next step. After doing this, you will most definitely be able to rise up and shine, improve, and succeed in life.

Change is seldom easy, but it's a big part of life, and you must accept and learn from it. It's like a marriage that ends in divorce. It's hard to take a step back, gain perspective, and understand why you are going through something so painful. You have to remind yourself that maybe it's because the love of your life is just around the corner, and if you'd stayed in a loveless marriage because it was comfortable or whatever, you never would have opened this new door and experienced true love. In the end, change brings positive results if you are willing to learn from it.

After opening and closing all these doors, my biggest lesson was learning how to downshift and accept the slower pace of my life. This drove me nuts at first. I was used to going a thousand miles an hour, and suddenly my career came screeching to a halt. So now what? I needed and missed the speed, so adapting to this change was far from easy. It took time and lots of thinking and analyzing, but in the end, I adjusted, and now I can see that it was necessary in my life.

The Past Is in the Past

Once you have taken the necessary time for reflection and the readjustment of your goals, it is time to look ahead. Don't get worked up about whatever happened in your life to bring on this change. Stop thinking and obsessing about the past and what could have happened if only you had done such and such a thing differently. It's too late. What's done is done. The past is in the past. This is the time to focus on what you can do from now on to feel better, to avoid making the same mistakes twice, to learn from the changes, and to apply these new lessons to your life.

If you hang on to the past, you'll continue to feel frustrated. And don't look to the sides, either; they're brimming with distractions. What you want is to stay focused on your present and future, always moving forward. That's why many racehorses have blinders, because if they look to the sides or behind them, they will get distracted, slow down, and probably lose the race. The same goes for us. Focus on yourself. Competition is important, but instead of competing with others, you should compete with yourself, with who you were last year and the previous one, to continue improving and outdoing yourself. That will motivate you and give you strength to approach the future with more energy and creativity.

> *Always try to be happy and at peace with your life.*

As you walk through each new door at every stage of life, never forget the main secret: Always try to be happy and at peace with your life. To find happiness, you must follow your heart. It sounds like a cliché, but at the end of the road you'll see it's true.

PUT IT TO WORK FOR YOU!

1. Don't let change get the better of you. When one door closes, another one opens.
2. Don't make decisions when your emotions are running high.
3. If you make a decision and notice it's not working out the way you had hoped, don't be afraid to leave that situation. There will be more doors to open.
4. Before crossing through another door into a new phase of your life, give yourself enough time to reflect and digest what just happened and plan your next steps carefully.
5. Once you're on track, avoid looking back and to the sides. The past is in the past; now you must focus on the present and future.

PART TWO

Relationships

12

Choose the Right Partner for the Journey

Your life partner can help you succeed in making your dreams a reality, or he can hold you back and limit you to a life that isn't even half of what you'd imagined. That's why it's so important to choose wisely when searching for the right person to share your lifelong adventures. Don't focus solely on his potential to be a good father or breadwinner. Also be on the lookout for a true partner—someone who supports your dreams, respects you, and knows how to share household responsibilities. Most important of all, before saying "I do," make sure you're motivated to marry by love, not out of convenience or need.

Chapter 5 covered the importance of investing in yourself. Well, choosing a good life partner is also an investment in you. Invest your time and heart in a man who loves you, desires you, and cheers you on, and steer clear of anyone who becomes an obstacle in your path. And, when you do ultimately choose a life partner, make sure your choice was made with an eye toward the future. It isn't necessary for the two of you to have similar interests—sometimes, it's actually better if you don't—but you ought to share the same bold dreams and goals and values. That way, the two of you will journey hand in hand on the road of life toward the same destination instead of pulling in different directions.

Sexual Attraction

One of the reasons you allow yourself to fall in love with someone is because you feel a sexual attraction to that person. That initial chemistry incites that special exchange of glances, which leads to that first date, the first kiss, and the first night together. Experiencing every one of these steps is essential in choosing the right partner. When Marcos and I got together, we fell head over heels. The attraction between us was tangible; we wanted to spend every minute together. Our chemistry was so strong from the get-go that we even thought it would be only a fleeting romance. We had no idea we were starting a relationship that is now celebrating its thirtieth anniversary. Yet that physical attraction is one of the secrets that has kept us together this long.

Knowledge Is Power

The chemistry between two people is so important that it is even defined by *Merriam-Webster's Dictionary*: "a strong mutual attraction, attachment, or sympathy."

Feeling mutual attraction is important, but so is being sexually compatible. That's right, you have to get along in life and in the bedroom—that physical compatibility is the essential foundation for an enduring relationship. People usually have very different sexual speeds. Some are slower and more relaxed, while others are like rabbits. If you're relaxed and you marry a rabbit, you will lose interest quickly. You have to find someone who's compatible in bed, who travels at your same speed. That's exactly why I don't think anyone should get married—ever— without having sex first.

Not only do I encourage you to make love before getting hitched, I also think it's essential for you to live with your future husband for a while, too. At the beginning of a relationship, you will each show your best side. The truth comes out when you live together. That's when you'll be able to see if he puts the cap on the toothpaste; if he watches sports all day; if he likes having sex once a day, twice a week, once a month, and so on. When you're sure the two of you are compatible both at home and in bed, then you can make a more informed decision about marriage.

Naturally, when I began to voice this opinion on my show, there was a huge uproar among all of the Latina mothers: "How dare you tell our girls to lose their virginity!" Hey, hold on, I'm not saying they shouldn't be virgins. All I'm saying is that if you are going to marry someone, you should make sure you are compatible. Would you buy a house or boat without stepping inside and seeing it? No, I didn't think so. And this isn't a piece of property we're talking about; the idea is for your relationship to last a lifetime. Take him for a spin, and if you don't like it, then move on to the next potential partner.

When you find that special person who makes your heart

SHARING THE TRUTH

At the beginning of our relationship, Marcos used to say that I thought of love and sex like a man: "So many men, so little time!" That changed when I met him, for one simple reason: I fell in love. Before that moment, I always thought that when you're loving someone, without being married or in a serious relationship, simply getting to know the person, with each new relationship you have with a possible partner, you are sharing your love. You're sharing a part of yourself in the most intimate way. During one episode of my show, Marcos and I sat next to each other and we let the audience ask whatever they wanted to know about us. And one person asked, "Cristina, were you a virgin when you got married?" To which I answered, "Yes, mami, both times."

pound, make sure he's fascinated by you too. Find someone who likes your body type and desires you just the way you are. There's nothing worse than being with a man who's constantly pointing out your flaws. If he keeps saying that you have to lose weight or change something else about yourself, it's pretty obvious: He's not that into you. To those who don't want to see it, I say open your eyes. It's as clear as day.

Some people don't have a specific body type they like, but they definitely have one they don't like. Don't get married to someone with a body that doesn't appeal to you, period. And beware: Sexual desire isn't exclusively physical. I know the attraction Marcos feels for me has to do with more than how I'm shaped or how much I weigh. He likes how I smell, how I talk, how I walk, and how crazy I can be. The fact that he's attracted to who I am as a person is an important factor that has led us to spend the last three decades together. So don't accept someone who isn't completely head over heels about you, and steer clear of the ones you don't adore. If you ignore this advice, you will regret it at some point.

Mutual Support

As a young woman, the worst discrimination I ever felt was at work. Women had to battle it out to get the respect we deserved at our jobs. Women today, especially Latinas, still face discrimination, but now it's not only at work, it's also at home. The traditional family structure still exists at home, where the man goes out to work and the woman supports him and manages all of the parenting and household responsibilities, too. The difference is that now women are also in the workforce and dreaming of having successful careers.

Therefore, questions from a husband such as, "Are my shirts ironed?" or "Where's my dinner?" become part of the daily discrimination a woman suffers at home when she doesn't choose a husband who is as supportive of her professionally as she is of him. When this happens, the number one saboteur isn't at work, he's at home, and now the real problem is you. If you choose someone who doesn't support your career, the one putting obstacles in your path is you and only you. If you find yourself in this type of situation, don't be afraid to make a change; it could be the best decision of your life.

My ex-husband didn't share my dreams of having a big life; he even thought the life and career goals I had were hurting our relationship, because he didn't believe they were attainable. I realized our ambitions and goals were different only after marrying him. And when I opened my eyes and felt that lack of support and how differently we perceived the trajectories of our lives, I knew this relationship wouldn't last much longer. Ending it wasn't easy, especially because we had a daughter, but ultimately it was the best decision I could have made. Closing that door gave me the space to open another one and find the right companion for my life's journey, who to this day supports everything I do.

When Marcos and I decided it was time for me to make the big move from magazines to television, for instance, our families were horrified and didn't believe we'd be able to make it work. Yet, with love and mutual support, we turned a deaf ear to their complaints and went after our dreams. Without that steady mutual support for each other, we probably wouldn't have had the strength to face our fear of change, defy our families, and go for something bigger.

That mutual support also helped us survive the enormous changes in our lives after we'd successfully reached our professional goals. We now live together, work together, and spend twenty-four hours a day together. It wasn't an easy transition, but we had one thing in our favor: I was ambitious and he was, too—for me! When Marcos urged me to pursue a career in television and I accepted his challenge, he had more faith in me than I did. To-

> *Mutual support is essential if you want to create and maintain a long, healthy, and happy relationship.*

gether we were able to succeed and achieve those big dreams that everyone else had doubted we'd ever reach.

To have a balanced marriage, you must select a partner who will support your goals and dreams, who will push you forward and celebrate your accomplishments as you do the same for him. Mutual support is essential if you want to create and maintain a long, healthy, and happy relationship.

Love and Respect

When I was younger, I didn't believe in love. I thought love was only for people who read romance novels. Because I had never fallen in love, I really didn't think it could exist. I continued to think true love was something I would never experience in my lifetime . . . until I met Marcos. In my thirties, I had managed to become the editor in chief of the second most important magazine in Latin America during a time in our history when women had to fight to be seen, treated, and recognized as equal to men. Love really wasn't on my radar. Even during my almost eight-year marriage with my first husband, I had never truly fallen in love. So, when that relationship ended, I simply didn't think love was in the cards for me. Since I had already achieved so many other important milestones in my life, and I was so grateful to have done that, I had come to accept that love wasn't part of my destiny.

I was on the loose for a year after my separation and when I met Marcos he was also going through a divorce. I had plenty of boyfriends and suitors, but with Marcos I found something special. Aside from the initial explosive attraction, with the passage of time Marcos showed me what it means to love. He opened my heart like no one else had ever done before, and taught me how to really cherish another person. I also learned how wonderful it is to mutually respect each other. Without that respect, everything else goes out the window. What's more, I let Marcos argue with me the way he does because I'm totally in love with him and I respect him as a husband, father, professional, friend, and person.

Marry for Love

One of the reasons my first marriage failed was because I didn't have my priorities straight. Ladies, if you get married only because you feel it's the right thing to do; because you've reached a certain age and it's expected; or because you need someone to support you financially, those are all the wrong reasons. Don't marry without love. It's that simple. And, please, make sure you're respected along the way.

> *Don't marry without love.*

I never understood trophy wives, the young and beautiful women who marry for money. First and foremost, don't marry for money, marry for love. But fine, let's say you're one of the few trophy wives who was truly in love when she got married, then, please, make sure your husband respects you. I don't see the purpose in marrying a rich husband just to spend his money on clothes. The guy married you to see you naked; he couldn't care less about your clothes. And a man who aims to climb the social ladder wants his wife to look refined and elegant, like Jacqueline Kennedy; he certainly doesn't want someone so sexy and provocative that the only thing she inspires is the arousal of his friends. So make sure you're respectable. Remember—love, respect, and mutual support are the key ingredients for a long-lasting relationship, as well as authenticity. Don't spend your life being the daughter, granddaughter, wife, or mother of so-and-so. Within all those roles you have to play in life, always maintain your individuality; if not, you will become invisible. No one deserves to be invisible in this world.

Many times, instead of looking toward the future, women focus too much on the present when they're trying to choose a life partner. Right, I get it. Who doesn't want her partner to dance well, have gorgeous eyes, and be romantic? That list of traits is a great big bonus. But you can't base your decision on that. You have to take into account your goals and dreams, where your boat is heading and where it will drop anchor. The key isn't to think about where you are today, but rather where you want to end up in life, so that both of you grow in that same direction. This is the foundation for choosing a long-term partner; if you don't share your final destination, your paths are bound to separate.

When I realized I didn't share my first husband's final destination, I got a divorce. Divorces are far from easy, even less so with a child. In my case, my daughter Titi was five years old. After a divorce, you are usually burned out and don't trust anyone. It's very hard to open up again with someone new. I spent some time when I didn't want to commit to just one man, so I tried a few on for size. When one of my lovers asked if I would consider marrying him, I immediately said no. I didn't want to marry anyone else again until Marcos came into my life. And trusting him was also difficult.

Marcos used to joke around and say, "Marry me now, you'll get a good deal, I'm on sale," because he was getting a divorce. And I used to laugh and think, *This guy is out of his mind*. Meanwhile, my mom said to me, "You're going to bring this guy home to live with your little girl? You don't even know him. He could be a child abuser!" And my dad said, "Don't marry someone eleven years younger than you; he'll only stick around for five." And I responded, "Yes, Dad, but those will be the five most delicious years of my life." Everything that crossed my mind and that I predicted came true, thank God, but instead of being the five most delicious years of my life, they turned into thirty, and we're still going strong!

Marcos is very mature; he has an old soul, and despite being eleven years younger than I am, he has always seemed eleven years older. In my first marriage, I wasn't happy because I didn't know what love was. Now I do know, and I hope no one misses out on such a wonderful feeling. That's why I always tell the women I meet that there's only one reason to get married . . . not two, not ten, just one: love. I've seen people marry for money, to climb the corporate ladder, or because they feel it's what they should do, but the only real reason you must have is that you're in love, hopelessly in love. Let me make myself crystal clear: Don't marry for money, and don't do it because the person satisfies all the requirements expected of a good man. Do it because you're so deeply in love that you can't imagine going through life without that person by your side.

PUT IT TO WORK FOR YOU!

1. If you don't have physical chemistry with a person, move on and find someone you're deeply attracted to. Chemistry isn't everything, but without it there's nothing.
2. Live with your partner before saying "I do," so you know beforehand what you're getting into.
3. Find someone who wants to support you as much as you want to support him.
4. Mutual support is one of the secrets to a long and happy relationship.
5. Don't look only for chemistry and love; also seek out mutual respect. It's another key to a long-lasting and healthy relationship.
6. Marry exclusively for love and love alone.

13
___

A Long-Lasting Couple
Evolves Together

I n the previous chapter, I shared my secrets to finding the right partner for your life's journey. Once you've found this person, you need to figure out how to make your relationship last. If you followed my advice, the two of you should already share your main goals and dreams, be in love, feel mutual attraction, and support each other. Now you must learn to continue evolving together and nourish the relationship so you don't lose each other along the way.

When you start a relationship, passion and attraction prevail. You then develop deeper feelings for the person and fall in love. Once you decide that's the person you want to spend the rest of your life with, you might marry, build a home together, have a family, and even enjoy grandkids. That's what most of us want in our lives, but how do you arrive at each of these stages? You must learn how to enjoy each year that passes, accept and support each other, share your challenges and successes, and grow together. If you fall, you have to know your husband will be there to pick you up, and you must do the same for him. It's not an easy journey, but it's a wonderful one when you have someone to share the good and bad along the way.

For a long-lasting marriage, make sure you:

- Evolve as individuals and as a couple
- Keep the flame of love alive
- Allow yourselves to fight and argue so you can learn and grow
- Don't lose your individuality along the way.

Each journey and couple is different, and as a couple, you must choose the route that calls to you both. The marriages of Celia Cruz and Pedro Knight and of Gloria and Emilio Estefan, are rock solid and lasted many years within the volatile entertainment business we're in. Celia and Pedro were together until the end, and Gloria and Emilio are still together after more than thirty years. Those two couples have been an amazing example throughout my life, and I'm proud to say that Marcos and I, too, are now among the few couples in the entertainment world that have managed to beat the odds and stay together for such a long time. What I'm about to share with you in the following pages are the amazing lessons I've learned on my journey with Marcos so far—lessons we've absorbed as we celebrate our thirtieth wedding anniversary.

Don't Get Left Behind

One of the easiest ways to grow apart from your partner over the years is for one of you to get left behind when it comes to your personal development. Typically, the man continues to grow and learn; advancing in his career, he's out there trying to make his dreams come true. The woman should do the same. Nourishing and developing yourself as a person will help nourish and develop your relationship with your husband. Don't lose the ability to hold a conversation with your husband that goes beyond what to buy at the market or what your kids are up to. Communication in a relationship is essential, and if you don't feed your soul with new information to continue learning, there will come a time when you won't have much to say.

> Nourishing and developing yourself as a person will help nourish and develop your relationship with your husband.

Stay informed. Read the newspaper from cover to cover and stay in tune with what's happening in your city, country, and the world. With this simple act, you'll have more topics to discuss not only with your husband, but also with business partners and friends—both his and yours. In addition, continue developing your career and hobbies; this will also give you something to talk about at the end of the day when the children are asleep. For instance, I love the passion Marcos has for koi fish. He talks to me about the fish and their Japanese history with such love that he makes me want to jump on a plane and fly to Japan with him to explore his passion. Supporting each other in what you do is important, as well as showing interest in what the other person is learning and developing during your free time. Add this to good communication and you've got a match made in heaven.

However, staying in step with your husband doesn't mean you have to start competing with him to see who has the last word. This isn't a game to see who wins; this is a tool so you can continue to be interested in each other. Actually, I don't want you to compete with any man. They aren't the enemy. Men are your allies. Focus on yourself and continue evolving as a person, so that you'll always have things to discuss and stimulate your relationship.

Keep the Flame Alive

Another big secret for a long-lasting relationship is to never let the flame between the two of you die out. Relationships change and evolve. With time, new things take priority over the old, but it's important to always fan the flames of attraction between you and your husband and keep them burning bright.

Marcos and I still go out on dates and nurture our life as a couple. We laugh, cuddle, and give each other gifts. Each of us knows what we must do to keep the other one interested, so please don't toss aside your sensual life; that attention and care you offer each other will help maintain your deep connection.

I'm very open-minded when it comes to love and sexuality, but I believe infidelity in general is equivalent to a lack of loyalty. It has nothing to do with sex; it means you're being disloyal to your best friend. And you know what? If you're ready to do that, just leave. No one deserves that pain. However, given all this talk, please don't feel pressured to be perfect so that your husband doesn't take off with another woman. That doesn't work, either.

For example, I don't wear makeup at home or to go run everyday errands. To me, makeup is for work or for parties. I use it when I'm giving an interview because I believe the person who came to see me didn't come to see Mati (my nickname); that person came to see Cristina. This doesn't mean I'm not vain, or that I don't feel good about myself. Makeup isn't the key to making you look beautiful. And I'm confident enough to say that I look great without it. I think women who depend too much on makeup to feel good are somewhat insecure. If this is your case, set your makeup aside and start building your self-confidence. You have no idea how sexy it is for a man to have a self-confident woman by his side.

There are many ways to look good, and you know what? You also look fantastic in your pajamas in your bedroom, with a freshly washed face, just like I think Marcos looks good while wearing workout clothes. The other night, we were getting ready for bed and I had zero makeup on. I asked Marcos, "Don't you love my nose?" mainly referring to the fact that my face wasn't powdered. And he answered yes. I not only believed him but I felt beautiful too. You don't have to put makeup on to look and feel your best. Self-confidence is all you need. And that's why I know my husband isn't going to satisfy himself somewhere else because I don't wear makeup. Besides, if he does, I'll kill him, and he knows it.

A piece of advice I gave to the women at *Cosmo* as editor in chief was the following: You wear perfume when you go out . . . put it on before going to bed. I sometimes spray so much perfume on my pillow and body that Marcos asks, "Well, what are you wearing today?" But the truth is he loves it when I smell good in bed. Who wouldn't? He also takes a daily shower, shaves, and uses his cologne, whether he has to leave the house or not.

Nothing is more pleasant than smelling good, and it's something we've both had in common since the start. It's so intoxicating! Although we both have a variety of colognes and perfumes, we love it so much that we give each other new bottles for our birthdays or on Christmas. This way, we not only continue to try new fragrances, but also nurture one of the ingredients that helps keep the flame between us burning brightly through the years.

> *You wear perfume when you go out . . . put it on before going to bed.*

You should also pay attention to what the other person likes. Do you know what my husband says when I wake up in the morning? He says I have the hair of an old rock-and-roll musician, like Mick Jagger. Of course, he's bald, so he loves my hair. And when it's tangled and tousled, it drives him crazy. You never really know what pleases the other person until he tells you. And so we circle back to the most important tool in any relationship: communication. You have to talk openly with each other. You can't guess what the other person likes, and you can't expect him to know what you like if you don't tell him. Talk! Share your preferences, and then remember that conversation so you can put it to good use when romance strikes.

Fighting Is Healthy

I think I've made it pretty clear that communication is essential in a relationship, but there are different ways to express yourselves. You can communicate through conversations about your interests and passions, by explaining what you like and dislike,

SHARING THE TRUTH

I recently had a sexologist as a guest on my radio show, and I discovered that there are way too many people who are scared to tell their partners, "Listen, I don't like that." You have to feel secure and comfortable enough to express what you like and dislike in bed. This won't only help you feel more satisfied, it will also make your husband feel better knowing that he's giving you what you need to feel pleasure. And if he doesn't listen and you aren't able to communicate and he isn't satisfying you, stop, toss him out, and find someone new. As the sexologist on my show so wisely said, "Love is forever, but not every love is forever." And let me add the following: To stay with the person you love for the rest of your days, you must communicate well in life and in bed.

by making love, and through fights. I know, that last one sounds strange, but it's true. Many times, you can learn a great deal when you disagree and, if you use this unpleasant moment in your favor, the issues that come up during arguments can help you evolve as a couple. Fighting is another way of communicating, and I think it's essential in a relationship.

I'm not trying to convince you that fighting is fun. It isn't. Usually it's ugly, tough, and emotionally stirring. But that's the secret: It stirs you on a deep emotional level when someone you love disagrees with you. It moves you and makes you learn about things that, if you hadn't argued, might not

> *Fighting is another way of communicating, and I think it's essential in a relationship.*

have ever come to light. And we evolve by learning. So, please, don't be fooled by those couples that say they never fight. That's a big fat lie! Or, if by some chance it is true, they probably won't last much longer together. When you lose interest in fighting with your partner, it means you've probably lost interest in that person, because you fight to emphasize your point of view, to be heard and respected. And that's all normal and healthy.

To get the response I need when I ask this question in an interview, I word it as follows: "When you fight, what's it usually about?" This way, the fighting is already implied, because you're not going to make me believe otherwise. And that whole never-go-to-sleep-angry advice is practically impossible to sustain over time. When Marcos and I are hell-bent in our arguments, we may fight for a couple of days straight before finally making up. If this happens, we still lie on the same bed at night, but since we're angry, Marcos draws an invisible line on the bed with his hand and says, "This is my side, and that's yours, so don't cross this line." And boy do we respect it! However, in the end, we manage to learn from these confrontations—and that's essential. That's why I always say that, in thirty years of marriage with Marcos, one of our secrets has been fighting, and fighting often, because that's when everything comes out in the open: the good, the bad, and the ordinary.

Growing up, I observed how my mom and dad adored each other and fought often. And they had an amazing relationship. My mom was the type of woman—and there probably aren't many like her—who cared more about her husband than her children. The Latina woman is usually quite the opposite. My mom and dad were intense. They fought, dear God, all the time.

If my mom went out of town to, say, North Carolina with her friends and my parents were in the middle of a fight, you can bet my dad would be there two days later to argue some more. It was what united them most. So much so, that when my dad died, he was lying on the ground after his heart attack, and my mom, who already had Alzheimer's, approached him, tapped him with her foot, and said, "Bebo, you weren't supposed to die before me. I'm older than you. Who am I going to fight with now?" They got married at twenty and were together for fifty years, constantly fighting and loving each other.

Individuality Is Part of the "We"

Over the years, a couple evolves together and becomes a "we." That "we" is a very special union that makes you feel like you and your husband will be together through thick and thin until the end. This "we" is truly beautiful and must be nourished and maintained. But I think many times that "we" can be misinterpreted. You shouldn't lose yourself in that "we"; it should complement your life. Becoming a "we" doesn't mean you leave your identity or individuality behind. On the contrary, you should continue developing that "we" as well as your personal desires and goals. Don't set aside what makes you feel good to become a "we." The idea is to join forces, rather than replace one for the other.

It really bothers me when people say "You have to find your other half." What do you mean? Are you

> *Becoming a "we" doesn't mean you leave your identity or individuality behind.*

implying that if I don't find a partner, I will never be complete? No way! You are not half of anything. You are complete, just the way God intended. When one complete person meets another complete person and they evolve as a couple, they create a "we." Each partner in that couple is still a special individual who has much to offer the other, and that's why one plus one is so much more than two.

To maintain that individuality within a couple, the secret is to give each other space to grow. As human beings, we are constantly growing, experimenting, learning, changing, and that's what makes a person interesting. If we didn't have all that, we'd just go to work, eat, and sleep. The curiosity you have about life and the urge to keep learning are what make you interesting.

As I've mentioned previously, supporting each other's interests is also imperative. Marcos developed a new hobby a few years back with koi fish, and today he spends a lot of his time learning all he can about them. I not only give him the space to do that, I support him. Seeing his passion for these fish doesn't bother me; it makes me happy. I like watching my husband's passion for what he does because it inspires me to do the same with my own interests. Likewise, he respects the time I spend researching my areas of interest or reading for pleasure.

Developing your personal interests is part of your individual growth, which in turn enriches your relationship. With personal evolution, you mature as a married couple. You learn how to respect each other's space and mutually support each other. Yes, mutual support, the basic secret we explored in the previous chapter, is definitely worth repeating here. Encouraging individuality in a relationship doesn't mean that your personal wants and needs take priority over mutually supporting each other. In other words, if Marcos doesn't play tennis, he's devastated. He loves it, but as I write this chapter, I'm sitting in a wheelchair because I slipped and fell in the bathroom and broke my foot. So Marcos, who plays tennis three times a week, is now here by my side, bathing me, taking care of me, and bearing with me instead of running off to the tennis court. Without thinking twice, he set that aside to take care of me, because now it's my turn. And when he gets one of his backaches, I also set aside my hobbies to help dress him and alleviate the pain.

So, you should give each other space to develop your own personal interests, but also set them aside if one of you needs help and support. That's basic. And the building block for it all is love. You really have to love the other person. That person you chose to be with for the rest of your life shouldn't only be your lover, he should be your best friend, and that's how best friends treat each other.

> *That person you chose to be with for the rest of your life shouldn't only be your lover, he should be your best friend.*

Individuality and the concept of "we" can also be applied to your friendships. I've seen endless numbers of people giving up close friendships because once they get married, all they do is go out with other couples. That's fun and all, but what happens if you don't like your husband's friend's wife? Either you stop seeing that couple, or you continue seeing them but you don't have a good time. However, there's a third possibility: encouraging each other to maintain your individual friendships. For example, if Marcos has a friend who's married to a woman with whom I have nothing in common, then he goes out with his friend, but we don't go out as couples, and vice versa. He has his friends and I have mine, because we have friendships we have made throughout the years that neither of us should have to give up because we've turned into a "we."

Sharing dreams and goals doesn't mean you have to share *everything*, only the most important and life-defining ones. If you have everything in common, there's a problem. One of you is probably lying and not being genuine. Learn how to differentiate between the goals and dreams you truly share and the ones you don't, and support and respect each other along the way. I feel completely satisfied with what I've accomplished with Marcos because being married to my second husband for three decades is a great achievement, especially since we also work together. And I couldn't have done it with a better person by my side. Now I know how important it is to choose the right partner for the journey, the person who I can share my dreams with, as well as my saddest moments, my accomplishments, and the happiest moments of our lives. If I had to do it all over again, I'd choose Marcos again in a heartbeat to share these past thirty years and the thirty to come.

> *Sharing dreams and goals doesn't mean you have to share everything.*

PUT IT TO WORK FOR YOU!

1. Don't set aside your personal development just because you're married. This will not only affect you, but also your relationship.
2. Keep the flame alive and don't be afraid to speak up and tell your partner what you like and dislike in bed.
3. Don't be afraid to fight with the love of your life. Just make sure you learn something from the situation so you can use it to evolve as a couple.
4. The person you have by your side should be your lover and your best friend.
5. Enjoy being a "we," but don't lose your individual self along the way.

14

You Can Have a Family and a Career

One of the questions I'm most frequently asked is how I managed to juggle both a successful career and a family. Many believe that you can really have only one or the other, but it's not possible to have it all. Well, I'm here to tell you that you can. I'm living proof. It's not an easy road, but no road worth traveling is easy. Combining a career with family life requires sacrifices and hard work, and some days you will be exhausted, but it's worth it in the end. Working outside the home allows you to take care of your family in the best possible way. And having a family gives you the love and support that a career will never be able to offer. At the end of the day, you can't hug a career.

> **At the end of the day, you can't hug a career.**

That phrase is one I use often, ever since it first came to me years ago while having a conversation with Sara Castany, my friend and *Vanidades* editor in chief. She said, "Matusi, how can you think about becoming pregnant again, now that Titi is already eight years old? Do you know what it means to start from scratch again, with another pregnancy, with small children, when your daughter is already past that stage? Enjoy your new marriage, don't be foolish." And I said, from the bottom of my heart, "When you're older and retire, you won't be able to hug a career. A career is a thing, not a person. And I need love in my life, from children, from grandchildren. I need to have a family." I come from a big family. I'm the oldest of five children and I have countless cousins. I knew one of my goals was to have my own family, and that's exactly what I did.

Wanting to start a family doesn't mean you have to put your career behind you. It's possible to find a balance, provided you find a good partner who will share the parenting and household responsibilities. If you have a good partner in crime you will be able to get rid of the guilt that comes with wanting to do both things, and you'll understand that you can have it all, just not at the same time.

Your Dreams and Your Family

Whether you have a husband, a husband and children, or you're single, as a woman you must follow your dream. Don't give this up when you get married or have children. It's possible to have both. Think about it: No man is ever asked if he's going to stay home and take care of the kids. Men are raised to follow their dreams and find a career, and that's what they do, with or without a family. Women must do the same thing. Achieving your dreams and goals also has positive repercussions for your family, because you will be happy with your accomplishments and your success will, in turn, help you provide your loved ones with better opportunities and care.

Children learn by example, not by words. By continuing to advance my career while raising my children, I set an example for them. Now my two daughters also have families and careers because they saw it was possible. In addition, Marcos and I have managed to maintain a strong and healthy relationship for over thirty years—no easy feat, especially in our industry. That has also set a wonderful example for our children regarding how to choose a partner and make your marriage last through the years. The way you live your life will set an important example for your children. Wouldn't you like them to follow their dreams and have a family? Show them it's possible through your actions.

> *The way you live your life will set an important example for your children.*

Clearly, in order to balance your career and family, your partner must be willing to support you in every aspect of your life along the way. For example, my daughters Titi and Stephanie both have husbands who are great in the kitchen. I do, too, and I'm thankful for that, because the art of cooking is definitely not my forte. As Marcos says, "The women in my family are lazy in the kitchen." Even my son, Jon Marcos, cooks. The fact is, if you have a career and children, it's essential that you and your partner complement and help each other out: While one cooks, the other one picks up around the house; while one does the laundry, the other folds and puts away the clean clothes, and so forth. You need to have someone by your side who supports your efforts, which goes back to my point in the previous chapters: You must choose your partner wisely. Don't pick someone based on how the two of you are living in the present day; you have to think about the goals and future he wants and if those match your own. In other words, you have to travel in the same direction, because if you don't, it's unlikely you'll make it to even five years of marriage, never mind last for decades, believe me.

Here's another secret to help you combine your dreams with your family: Finding and investing in excellent child care is almost as important as finding a good life partner. One of the wonderful benefits for anyone with a large, close family is that we can count on grandmothers, aunts, and cousins or even second cousins to help us take care of our children. Every professional woman who can count on such a large family, which includes relatives and friends, has a gold mine of unconditional love and support. If this is your case, take advantage of it and thank your lucky stars every day, because not everyone can bank on such a luxury.

Not having family nearby to help you with the children makes it harder to raise your family while forging a career, but not impossible. You simply have to do some research in your social circles to get a good recommendation for a nanny or day care provider. For example, if you decide to hire a nanny, find two or three candidates and interview them. I suggest you meet them at their homes, since seeing how they live can be revealing. Once you choose the best candidate for your family, give her a trial run to see how she gets along with your children.

Keep in mind that often a nanny who takes care of your children has had to leave her own children with another woman in her native country to come here, make a better living, and give them what they need. This chain creates what, ideally, should be one of the most beautiful examples of feminism: Two women mutually helping each other to support their families. One works to support her family and pursue a career, the other is here in the United States because she needs money to maintain her family, but they are like sisters because they're essentially doing exactly the same thing—taking care of their families. When Titi was a little girl, I made a deal with a Colombian woman: Since she took care of her grandchild so her daughter could work, I hired her daughter at the magazine, then hired the woman and let her bring her grandchild to my apartment, where she took care of him and my daughter. We helped each other out and both came out stronger for it.

Again, it's yet another road that's not easy for any woman. I know it broke Stephanie's and Titi's hearts when they first had to leave their babies in someone else's care, just like it will hurt the first time they have to leave them at preschool or the first time they have a nanny they don't know. Every parent dies a little in those moments—I know I sure did. When I had Titi, I didn't have money to hire a nanny, so I put her in the baby car seat, ate a sandwich in the car—because I didn't have time for lunch or dinner—dropped her off with whomever was taking care of her, and went back to work on my nightly freelance projects.

If you don't have access to a good nanny, there are alternatives. One of my daughters, who was lucky enough to have a six-month maternity leave, found the best day care for her child when it was time for her to return to work. Just like when you're choosing a babysitter or nanny, before choosing a day care, make sure you do the necessary research to find the one that best fits your needs. Search online for places with good reviews and ask other parents for recommendations. Then, visit the places you've narrowed down so you can choose the one you like the most. Our daughter did it and now her child is happy and her mind is at ease.

There are different solutions and combinations that you can find if you don't have money or family nearby. You have to be flexible, creative, and open-minded to actually notice the different possibilities and options. Sometimes the answer is right in front of your nose, but you can't see it. Open your eyes and check out whatever is within reach. If you do, you'll find some sort of solution.

Knowledge Is Power

Go online and search for child care within your city. I did a general search and found this site, Baby Center, that may give you more tips regarding work and pregnancy, as well as other baby-related subjects: www.babycenter.com.

Most women today work and have a career, because today's economy demands that both people in a couple work to support their family. Few women can afford to stay home full-time with their children. If you are part of the majority of women who work, remember that finding a good child-care solution is an amazing investment, because it will put your mind at ease and will give you the necessary time to advance on the job, reach your career goals, and give your family the financial support they deserve.

Kick Guilt and Resentment to the Curb

I never felt guilty, nor do I regret having a career and a family, but since machismo and male chauvinism are still present in our society, guilt and resentment are still a problem for many working women today.

SHARING THE TRUTH

I've had to deal with a lot of stuff throughout my life, and I think the one thing I've never gotten over is machismo. I have nothing against men, but rather against machismo. The first time I felt the effects of true machismo was during a trip to Morocco five years ago. I bought a dreamlike tour—it seemed like it was straight out of *One Thousand and One Nights*—and when we arrived, our guide and driver were promptly waiting to take us to our first stop. The guide didn't speak to me. He turned his back to me. I would enthusiastically mention something that I wanted to do, and he didn't even look at me. I walked around him and talked to him face-to-face, asking that he please not be so disrespectful, but he didn't even acknowledge my existence. Never in my life have I felt machismo so blatantly. I was nothing, invisible.

Machismo in Latin America and the U.S. isn't as obvious as the kind I felt in Morocco, but it still exists. I've fought against that kind of invisibility all my life, but today's women seem like they've given up. The problem with some young women today is that they're too preoccupied about their bra sizes, how they look in a swimsuit, how to avoid gaining weight, how to fight aging and marry someone who will take care of their problems, instead of figuring out how to solve them on their own. They're still stuck there. Too many generations have been brought up with this same behavioral pattern and we need to keep fighting to eliminate it once and for all.

However, our twenty-first-century reality requires that both people in a couple get jobs in order to educate their children, own two cars, and allow themselves some luxuries. When I was younger, the big argument was between the women who worked and those who stayed at home. Working women were considered bad mothers, bad wives, bad at everything, while those who stayed home to raise their children were considered virtuous and good in all they did.

That dichotomy practically doesn't exist anymore, but there's still an essential problem. All mothers, the women raising men and women of the future, have a huge responsibility: We must raise our children to reject machismo. This change must come from within our own families for it to finally be reflected in societies throughout the world. And to attain this, we must return to basics: You must carefully choose your life partner. Find a man who is willing to support, encourage, respect, and help you, and will instill these values in your children. The wrong person will not only make you feel guilty; he may also pass on those feelings of guilt and resentment to your children.

When both parents pursue careers, the biggest challenge is to banish guilt when it comes to the children. Your children may feel abandoned when you go off to work, and they'll make you feel it. Instead of being guilt-ridden and anxious, try to remind them that you are still present in their lives—even though you go to work, you always come back—and take pictures of whatever you do together. The last may sound like strange advice, but you have no idea how much pictures have helped me with my children. When Jon Marcos used to say things to me like, "Oh, I remember when my grandmother took me to my first haircut," instead of feeling bad and trying to convince him that wasn't the case, I'd show him a picture and reply, "No, honey. This was your first haircut. You were six months old, we were at home, and I was the one who cut it." Many times our children forget what you actually did do with them, so gentle reminders, such as photos, can be a useful and welcome tool.

Another way of dealing with this possible resentment from your children is to make them understand why you work, which you can do as follows: First, make sure you make work a family affair; and second, remind them that the entire family will benefit from your huge effort.

Work Is a Family Affair

Regardless of where you work and what career path you're in, always make sure it's a family affair, like we did. By doing so, your entire family will be able to understand that everything you do, you do for them as well as for yourself. That way they'll feel that, by supporting you, they're doing their part in helping everyone in the family. When you turn your career into a family affair, the resentment your child, or even your own parents, will feel over how hard you work will lessen.

> *Regardless of where you work and what career path you're in, always make sure it's a family affair.*

We always told our children that this business their parents had is ours, it's a family business, and we backed this statement with action. Let me give you an example. Anyone who knows me knows that I have fought hard on behalf of gay rights and AIDS awareness and research. My brother and sister are gay, and thank God I experienced it in the flesh, because that educated me on the subject. While doing my show, we dedicated an episode to gay marriage and had gay couples get symbolically married on the set. We did this before anyone else, before Oprah Winfrey, before Barbara Walters, before anyone. In response to that episode, fifteen hundred Christian fundamentalists took to the streets to protest. One of their banners read, YES TO CHRIST, NO TO CRISTINA! During all that turmoil, my son turned to me and asked, "Mami, what does *gay* mean?" And I replied, "It's like having blond or brown hair, having light- or dark-colored eyes, being tall or short." So he said, "Oh, that's it?" To which I responded, "Yes."

However, before taping that particular episode, I had gathered my family and asked, "Are you okay with this program I'm planning to do?" They all said yes, that it was a family affair, and they supported me because they agreed that I was right in doing such a show. That was crucial to me, because they also had to suffer the consequences of all the people picketing against me. It made me think of how my mom and dad might feel, being old and devout Catholics, or how my children would feel at school when they were insulted due to what I did on the show. Yet, by asking for their blessing, their participation made us feel like we were a united front fighting for the same cause. You have to fight for what you believe in, and in an industry that is so public, I needed my family's support and wanted to make sure they knew that this business was theirs, too.

Your Career Benefits Your Family

If you think about it, your entire family benefits from your career, not just you. How can the chance to help your loved ones by working so hard make you feel guilty? That huge effort you're making is opening the way for your children to be able to achieve their dreams, and it's giving you the possibility to support your family in the best way conceivable.

In many families, the children have dreams, but they don't have the opportunity to study to reach those dreams. Things have changed quite a bit since I was young, such as the economy. Now, if both parents don't have jobs, it becomes very difficult to make enough money to educate their children through college. It's important we do everything in our power to help our youth get educated and pursue their dreams.

Thankfully, there are several ways to save for your children's education. You can open a college fund while they're just toddlers and start saving for their college educations. Deposit whatever you can afford into that account on a monthly basis, so that when your children are ready for college, they'll have something to start off with. You'll have to be disciplined, but you can do it. On the other hand, if your child has a particular talent or does very well in school, he or she will have access to a wide variety of grants and scholarships. Financial aid is also available to residents within each state. Anything is possible if you set your mind to it and take action.

Knowledge Is Power

MeritAid.com is an online directory of merit-based scholarships and academic scholarships from colleges across the country. Ask your child's high school counselor for more information.

Our hard work allowed us to give our children the best educations. When the time came for each of them to head off to college, they were able to choose the majors they desired, and we were able to pay the tuition bills and help set them off on their own journeys toward their goals and dreams. Thanks to the sacrifices I made for work, I was also able to take care of my parents when they got old; I hired nurses to look after my mother when she got Alzheimer's. And, when my son was diagnosed with bipolar disorder, I was able to find him the most qualified doctors and get the best available treatment.

The secret to battling the guilt you might feel as a working mother who has to leave her family for hours each day is to remind yourself what you're working for. You're not taking anything away from anyone by working; you're adding to the family's common good. Remember this at all times, but especially when you feel guilt creeping up on you. You work to support and give your family opportunities to get ahead, and, if they haven't yet done so, each and every one of them will thank you for it one day.

Hiring and Working with Friends and Family

Many people don't believe in hiring friends or family, but I disagree. You have to choose who you employ well, and it's a delicate balance, but hiring people you know and trust can be done and may provide the most fruitful relationships imaginable. Being a boss is a difficult job, and being a friend or family member's boss also has its challenges, but if you have good communication skills and there's a similar work ethic, it can be a positive experience. Actually, if you work with a group of people for a long time, like Marcos and I have done, you end up caring for them and feeling like they've become part of your family. If you spend many hours at work, sometimes you see your employees and colleagues more than your own children, so creating that bond with them is inevitable.

> *You're not taking anything away from anyone by working; you're adding to the family's common good.*

Today, things that affect our work family affect us, and if we can help them, we do so in the blink of an eye. That instinct, born of affection, creates a sense of loyalty that can be an enormous bonus within the work relationship. I consider my employees who invest in their careers and have goals and passions as work colleagues, not just employees. We share similar dreams, we care for each other and watch each other's backs . . . we're like family. For instance, Jorge Insua has been working with us for more than twenty years, and I no longer see him as an employee or even as a friend; nowadays, he's like a son to me. We share our sorrow and happiness and support each other in all we do. Don't underestimate those work relationships, because many will become lifelong friendships.

And as for my family and friends, I clearly have a lot and can't hire them all, because many don't have the interest or skills to work in this industry. That said, if you have friends or relatives who do have the potential to fill certain positions, they're prudent and won't take advantage of the situation, and you can easily and openly communicate with them, why not hire them? My brother Iñaki is my assistant and works with us every day. Aside from being an excellent person and an amazing human being, he's an incredible employee and we share a similar work ethic. The same goes for my cousin Maritere. That's why I insist, from experience, that you shouldn't rule out hiring relatives and friends because they might make fantastic colleagues.

Another issue I hope we all keep in mind when hiring new employees is age-based discrimination. There are many qualified candidates that may not be as young as others, but don't forget that age brings with it a wealth of experience. Marcos, for example, has an accountant who's eighty-five years old and doesn't use a computer—and it should be noted that Luisa was our friend before becoming our accountant. She does everything by hand, old-school, and she's better than many in her industry. Aside from admiring Luisa because she's completely competent professionally, Marcos loves her like a mother, and when he talks with her, often she gives him magnificent advice. Why? Because she has years of experience. So, when it's time to hire people, always keep in mind that your relatives and friends could become amazing colleagues.

Can You Have It All?

What I tell women who want to have a career and a family is: Yes, you can have it all, just not at the same time. Life is made up of a series of stages and, to achieve all you set out to do, you must adjust to each stage accordingly. If you do, at the end of the road you'll be able to look back and say you did it all. In my case, one of the things I most enjoy at this stage of my life is spending time with my children and grandchildren. My daughter came over yesterday with my grandchildren and she brought a dozen sticky buns, and we ate them all! I wasn't able to share moments

> *You can have it all, just not at the same time.*

like this in the past, because I was working and constantly watching what I ate, but yesterday I was able to savor that delicious treat with my family and enjoy every second of it.

Life is full of difficult choices. Regardless of your career or industry, there will always be a price to pay for following a certain path. You will miss a birthday or have to reschedule events; it happens to the best of us, but women suffer the consequences more than men because we still live in a chauvinistic world. Everything has a price or requires a sacrifice, and the key to making the right sacrifice is to figure out what it is so you can face it and get it over with sooner rather than later. By doing so, you can move on to the next stage and be closer to your main dream.

One day, many years ago, when our children were still teenagers, Marcos walked into Jon Marcos's room and found the three of them talking about what they could possibly do to surpass all of our accomplishments. At the time, my show was at the height of its success, as were we. Marcos realized they were worried, so he sat down with them and explained that our goal was for them to choose what they wanted to do in life and be happy with their decisions. He explained that we didn't want them to study a specific career or follow in our footsteps because each one had to find his or her own calling. And he reassured them that we would be proud of what each one of them accomplished in their lives, no matter what career paths they chose. They have to live their own lives, that was our goal; it's what we most wanted for them. That's why we worked so hard: We wanted to give them the chance to follow their own dreams and support them along the way. And that's what happened. Now we have wonderful grandchildren and our children have become our friends. We share advice, sorrow, happiness, and beautiful family moments. And that is one of the most important benefits we have reaped from our decision to have both a family and a career.

PUT IT TO WORK FOR YOU!

1. Don't set aside your dreams to get married and have kids. You can have both.
2. The way you handle your life will be a lasting example and point of reference for your children.
3. Finding child care that fits your needs is one of the best investments you can make for you and your family.
4. Show your kids that your business is also theirs and let them know how they will benefit from all your hard work, so you can eliminate the guilt and resentment that having a career and a family can cause.
5. Always remember that you can have it all, just not at the same time.

15

Mental Illnesses Are Serious:
Don't Ignore the Signs

When you're feeling physically unwell, you go to a doctor so that he or she can help you feel better. Well, you must take care of your mental health in the same way. For example, if you're generally a positive person, but find you're dragging yourself out of bed and no longer want to engage in your usual activities, or if you're feeling sad all of the time and can't seem to stop crying, you may be depressed. If these feelings persist for several days in a row, seek professional help. Please don't ignore the signs, as it could quickly turn into a life-or-death situation. Find a psychologist or psychiatrist to help you identify the root of the problem and find a solution.

Knowledge Is Power

Psychologists and psychiatrists must be licensed professionals with a master's in psychology; however, psychiatrists have an additional seven years of medical education under their belts with a doctor of medicine degree. Therefore, psychiatrists, unlike psychologists, can prescribe medication to their patients.

Like most people, I have also experienced times when I've felt depressed, but not for the usual reasons. For example, lack of money doesn't depress me. Marcos scolds me, but I believe there's always a way to earn more money; the prospect of financial difficulty doesn't worry me as much as it might others, or even as much as it does Marcos. But, when I lost my job, that was a different story. I had spent twenty-one years in a place I considered home. The people I worked with and the company I worked for were like family. So, when the job I'd been doing for twenty-one years disappeared overnight, well, it shook me to the core. I fell into such a deep depression that I had no choice but to seek help. I went to see a psychiatrist.

SHARING THE TRUTH

Going to therapy doesn't mean you're crazy. We have to stop thinking that way. We all need help at some point in our lives to organize our thoughts and understand our emotions. Don't be afraid of therapy. It can be invaluable when you need it most. I've done quite a bit of therapy during my life. And each time, from each session, I have learned something that helped me evaluate what was happening in my life and arrive at new solutions to whatever challenges had brought me into therapy, so that I could continue my journey.

Therapy helps if you're feeling down, and so can exercise. If you're feeling sad or depressed, get up, get dressed, and take a walk. Eat healthier. Clear your mind and look for things to do that are good for your soul. Try not to feed into the depression, and instead do your best to short-circuit the cycle of sadness. However—and this is crucial—if nothing you do makes you feel better, *seek professional help*!

Aside from paying attention to your emotions and thoughts and treating your own mental health if necessary, it's also essential to keep an eye on each member of your family. My mother had Alzheimer's disease, but I didn't realize it until my father passed away because he was covering it up. And my son Jon Marcos is bipolar, but we had to reach a crisis point that I wouldn't wish on anyone before we finally understood he needed help. Don't ignore the signs. If something isn't going well with you or with someone you love, let me repeat: Seek professional help.

What follows is the story of my son Jon Marcos and a mental disorder that was advancing before our eyes without any of us noticing. My goal in sharing such an intimate family experience is to help you recognize when something isn't right with you or with someone you love, and to encourage you not to be afraid to ask for help. We should never have to feel ashamed if we suffer a problem with mental health. These conditions are like other illnesses, even if they're sometimes harder to diagnose. With the medications available today and a good medical team, it's possible to conquer the stigma and find the right treatment if mental illness affects you or a family member.

The Most Excruciating Moments of My Life

Jon Marcos was our family's golden child. He was so outgoing, amusing, intelligent, charismatic, and adorable that everyone in the entertainment industry wanted him to appear in commercials. He was never your run-of-the-mill child. He has always been an extremely observant and sensitive person, so much so that we used to call him "Truth Serum" because he couldn't lie. He was advanced for his age and the type of curious child who always asked incredible questions that were far more profound and insightful than those posed by other children his age. For example, when I started working in television, people sent me tons of flowers. They were enormous, all made of cut flowers. And Jon Marcos asked me one day, "Mami, why do you like dead things?" I looked at him and said, "Dead?" And he replied, "Those flowers are all dead; they stink. Why don't you ask people to send you flowers that are alive?" He was only five years old when he made that keen observation, and I took his advice. From that moment on, I always asked people to send me live flowers, especially orchids. Another time, while in the car with Marcos on our way to Miami Beach, Jon Marcos asked, "Papi, what did God die from? Because no one dies from having a few nails hammered into their hands."

At the beginning, Marcos and I were working nonstop on the daily TV show and on endless other projects designed to continue advancing our careers. Jon Marcos grew up with two workaholic parents. This wasn't something that pleased him, and he let me know how he felt about this on more than one occasion. For example, as a child, whenever he saw me wearing the makeup I put on for work, he'd look at me and say, "I'm not looking for Cristina; I want my mom." Much later, when he was sixteen, he came up to me and said, "I don't have a mom. My mom is a vegetable in a pressure cooker; I don't have a mother."

Things happen for a reason. Around the same time he made this pressure cooker comment, there was a shift in my work life that I now realize was the best possible thing that could have happened. That year, Univision called to say that, over time, *The Cristina Show* had become increasingly expensive to produce. Back then we were still taping a daily show, from Monday through Friday. When the executives proposed turning our daily show into a weekly one, we accepted, and the timing couldn't have been better.

I had noticed that, at sixteen, Jon Marcos was going through a stage that required us to give him more attention and be more present in his life. It wasn't enough to just take him to Disney or to L.A. on a work trip. I felt that I ought to spend more time with him, but I never imagined that, only three years later, our lives would explode like that pressure cooker he'd referred to earlier.

Jon Marcos had a beautiful girlfriend—I called her "Fairy Princess" because she was so gorgeous, with red hair cascading to her waist—and she was from Texas. They dated for about five years; with the Internet's help, they were able to maintain a long-distance relationship. But one day his girlfriend left him for another guy who lived in Texas, and this event caused something strange to grow within Jon Marcos, though in reality he had always carried the seed inside him.

In retrospect, I now believe my father may have been bipolar, but in Cuba at that time it was referred to as being manic-depressive, and nobody paid much attention to it. We knew my dad had highs where he felt like he could conquer the world, and lows where his sorrow consumed him, but we had no idea his mood swings derived from a mental disorder that could be treated. We just thought it was part of his personality. Once, when I was sixteen, I said to my dad, "I feel really bad. I want to see a psychiatrist." And he replied, "Honey, I feel so bad that if we had enough money to pay for a psychiatrist, I'd be the one going, not you." My dad's mood swings were incredible. In his case, he never tried to commit suicide, but he always said he wanted to die.

Jon Marcos had similar symptoms in terms of mood swings. In addition, he suffered from many social phobias, but I never saw these as something strange because I thought he'd inherited those social phobias from me. For example, I don't have a cell phone and I don't like speaking on the phone; I don't like being found. I'm also so claustrophobic that elevators make me panic. Similarly, Jon Marcos can't stand having too many people around. However, all parents know that every child has a unique personality, so I attributed his behavioral quirks to that.

One night, Marcos and I were attending one of the first in a series of events to be held in celebration of the Casa Cristina collection in Miami. We had reserved the most elegant hotel in Coral Gables and invited the presidents of every relevant company to spend that weekend with us celebrating the line with events and seminars. As we kicked off the weekend, at one point that evening I glanced at Marcos and realized from his expression that something was going on, but he didn't say anything. When the event was over, we got into our car and Marcos said, "Mati, I just got a call to tell me that Jon Marcos tried to commit suicide." I couldn't process what he was saying. Kill himself?

How? And why? I had met people on my show who had tried to commit suicide, but never anyone in my personal life. I couldn't make sense of it.

As we found out later, Jon Marcos had gotten into his car and driven to a parking lot's fifth floor, where he found himself wondering whether to jump or not. When he realized what he was thinking, he turned the car around, drove straight to the hospital, and checked himself in. In the middle of all this, we had to take our guests, who were back at the hotel, to South Beach to a Cuban dinner we had planned. My son was hospitalized because he had tried to kill himself, yet I had to dine and dance with these people because they were our guests who we had flown in.

First thing the next morning, I rushed to the hospital and met my brother Iñaki at the entrance. He was crying inconsolably. I remember noticing that the door leading to the psychiatric ward was made of steel; I supposed it was to prevent patients from escaping easily. When I saw my brother in that state, I said, "Why are you crying like this?" I wouldn't let myself cry; I was determined to act by taking control of the situation. I needed to see my son!

I rang the doorbell. When the door opened, I told the woman blocking my entrance that I was Jon Marcos's mother and I had come to request his release. From what I understood, since he wasn't an adult yet, they couldn't keep him there without my consent.

But she said, "Cristina, I want you to think hard about what you're asking, because your son is very sick."

"My son isn't very sick; he lives with me; he's fine," I said desperately.

"He obviously felt bad enough to come here on his own," the woman answered.

In any case, she didn't have the authority to release him. To sign him out, I had to go to the hospital psychiatrist's office. There, the psychiatrist told me that he thought Jon Marcos was bipolar, that he'd been suffering from this illness prior to this breakdown, and that he was now going through a strong episode triggered by the crisis of the breakup with his girlfriend.

Today I understand that, after his relationship with that girl ended, Jon Marcos fell into a deep depression that prompted this mental breakdown. That first suicide attempt was just the beginning. During the following weeks, we found him doing things like hiding knives under his pillow. His ex-girlfriend was concerned enough to call me and beg me to do something because she was so worried Jon Marcos might kill himself.

Not long after that first episode, I sat with my son in our garden at home and, as we watched the fish swim in the pond, we had a long conversation. His behavior up to that point had been very strange, but after talking to him he seemed calmer and that made me feel more relaxed. I thought our conversation had done him good because he seemed to be feeling better. However, when we entered the house, he didn't go into his room, but into mine. I thought that was odd, so I followed him. When I walked in, I saw that he had grabbed the bottle of sleeping pills Marcos and I had and emptied them all into his mouth, swallowing them without a drop of water. Marcos ran to the phone and called 911. Within minutes, the police and an ambulance arrived at our door; they put Jon Marcos on a stretcher, handcuffed him so he couldn't do himself more harm, and took him back to the hospital's psychiatric ward.

And so began our crusade through hospitals, psychiatrists, medicine, and anything else we thought might be the best treatment for Jon Marcos's bipolar disorder. We were constantly admitting and discharging him from the hospital as he suffered various crises, until finally realizing we needed a better solution. The hospital he was in at that moment was actually just a regular hospital with one floor dedicated to mental health patients. And, on that floor, many of those who came and went were homeless people. They were hospitalized, tranquilized with an injection, and then released. It became very clear to us that this wasn't an environment where Jon Marcos could get better.

We began doing more research on bipolar disorder to have a clearer idea of where to take him and how to help him. We wanted to understand what the hell was happening to our son. One day, I was returning from a business trip when I ran into Columba Bush, Florida governor Jeb Bush's wife, at the airport. I've known Columba for many years, and knew she had a daughter who'd battled addiction problems, so I explained what was going on with Jon Marcos. She immediately recommended La Amistad Behavioral Services outside of Orlando, Florida, one of the top mental health facilities in the country. Jon Marcos spent the next year-and-a-half there. Meanwhile, little by little, we continued searching for the best ways to treat his illness.

We finally found McLean Hospital in Belmont, Massachusetts, which specializes in treating patients with mental illnesses. The doctors there thoroughly examined Jon Marcos and he spent another few years at that institution. We visited him four times a year, and all along I was dying inside. I missed him horribly, yet I had to keep going on as if everything was normal. That was one of the most agonizing periods of my entire life. Jon Marcos is the baby of the family, such a good person, and we all adore him. At last, after so much back-and-forth, we began to detect an improvement.

How had we missed the fact that my son's mental health was deteriorating over the years? The signs were all there, yet we didn't recognize them. Perhaps if ours had been a more traditional family, his symptoms would have been more evident, but that wasn't the case. We live in a very creative world, surrounded by emotive and nontraditional artists, musicians, writers, and journalists. Jon Marcos grew up in this environment, and he was also different, intelligent, creative, and unconventional, so we never saw his behaviors as strange. We just thought he was eccentric.

Knowledge Is Power

According to the National Institute of Mental Health, approximately 26.2 percent of the U.S. population, eighteen and above, has some sort of mental disorder. In other words, one in every four adults suffers some type of mental illness. Bipolar disorder affects around 5.7 million adults in the United States.

We never imagined that something like this could happen in our family. At times, when you face a problem so enormous, you can enter a stage of denial that blinds you from seeing the obvious. It's a grave mistake to perpetuate this denial, since the only thing that does is aggravate the suffering of the person affected. By denying that a problem exists, you're also effectively denying your loved one the professional help necessary to recover.

I was one of these people at the beginning. I was in denial; I couldn't see my son's problem until it roared to life and bared its teeth. Then I had no choice but to accept what was happening and educate myself. It's important to educate yourself on these issues so you can recognize the symptoms and seek help before it's too late. This is the best possible scenario for the person suffering the illness as well as for family members, who suffer in a different way but also need support.

Knowledge Is Power

If you want to learn more about the different mental disorders that exist and their symptoms, visit the National Institute of Mental Health Web site: www.nimh.nih.gov.

Marcos and I decided to keep this family crisis quiet for a few years for several reasons. The pain was tremendous and we weren't interested in exploiting our family's experience to gain publicity. But the main reason was to give Jon Marcos a chance to go through this in private so he could recover in peace. When we finally made it public on my radio channel and in a *People en Español* column, I had first asked Jon Marcos if it would bother him if I spoke openly about his illness. And he said, "No,

> *Often we don't see the signs right in front of our eyes, or even if we do, we don't want to acknowledge them.*

Mami, everyone should know about this. If only we had known more ourselves." He's very selfless and sure of himself in this. Many times he has said, "We have to help people, because otherwise they might not know how ill they are."

When mental illness strikes a family, it has a tremendously profound and painful effect on everyone. You don't know what it's like to live with something like this until it touches you personally. When I was first told that Jon Marcos had attempted suicide, my initial reaction was, "No, that doesn't happen in Mati's house. This happens on *The Cristina Show.*" But yes, it *does* happen in Mati's house. Often we don't see the signs right in front of our eyes, or even if we do, we don't want to acknowledge them. I didn't think I was that kind of person, but it happened to me, too. We must open our eyes, be more observant, and remember that no one is immune to sickness, physical or mental.

First and foremost, we must abolish the myth that therapy is only for "crazy" people. The initial reaction when one person suggests that another should seek help from a psychologist or psychiatrist is often to say, "Hey, I'm not crazy." There's a stigma associated with the word "crazy." Listen, if your stomach aches for several days straight, wouldn't you go to your doctor to identify the cause and stop the pain? Well, the same should be true for your mental health. If you spend several days in an extremely emotional state or you're not behaving like yourself, you should also seek help. And I'm not talking about only serious mental issues. Life-changing events such as losing your job, getting a divorce, grieving for a loved one who has passed on, are very traumatizing, and therapy is usually a great support tool.

> *Don't be afraid to seek help and talk over your problems with a professional.*

Think about it this way: If your head hurts for several days in a row and you don't take anything for the pain, it could go away eventually, but you might suffer twice as much as if you'd gone to the doctor and asked for treatment. Likewise, if you feel emotionally unwell and ask for help, the time you spend feeling distressed will likely be shorter than if you don't seek treatment. Therapy is crucial. Accept it in your life as a tool that will help you process big changes and come out stronger. Don't be afraid to seek help and talk over your problems with a professional. Family and friends may have the best intentions, but they don't always know how to offer the right support, unlike professionals who dedicate their lives to helping others with their problems. And when something like what happened to Jon Marcos and us occurs, therapy is not only necessary for the person suffering the mental disorder, it's also crucial for the family supporting the patient. It provides you with the skills you need to more successfully cope with the situation and, in turn, this gives you the chance to offer support to your family member.

The Pain, the Guilt, and the Next Crisis

Our son's mental disorder caused me to suffer from a heavy heart and inexplicable pain. I felt the pain every moment, during the day, at night, at work, at home. It was years of constant pain. When I went to award shows and was asked, "So, Cristina, how does this recognition make you feel?" although I smiled and responded politely, what I truly felt was PAIN. Everything was pain. That feeling was constantly in my heart during those first years. It was so immense and deep that I thought it would never go away; however, when I saw signs of slight improvement in my son, I was finally able to see the so-called light at the end of that tunnel of agony.

In a situation like ours, with pain also comes guilt. One of the things you must confront and work through as the family of a person with a mental illness is that you're not to blame for this happening. Many parents may deny their child's problem because they believe that, if they admit it exists and seek help, they're also admitting that they did something wrong. This just isn't true. These illnesses, when caused by chemical disorders that affect the brain, simply happen. They aren't your fault; this is out of your hands.

To help alleviate your guilt, get more information on the disorder and talk with a professional. I'm still working on banishing my own guilt; it's not an easy road. It's hard for me personally because I see a lot of myself in Jon Marcos; I know where some of his phobias come from because they're mine. And yes, I feel guilty for having passed these things on to him. That feeling of being responsible for your child's mental distress is difficult to shake. That's why we've done several family therapy sessions with and without him. It's necessary to understand where the guilt comes from and confront it, get on top of it, and move on.

Many times, the guilt is present in the questions you ask yourself after traumatic episodes, especially when it has to do with your children: Did I do everything I could? Why didn't I spot the signs earlier? Could I have done something different? Did this happen because I wasn't at home and was working too much? But the past is in the past, and even psychologists will tell you there's nothing you can do to change the past. At the end of the day, many mental illnesses are the result of a chemical imbalance and that's it. We must focus on the present and the future, on doing everything we can to help the person we love get better.

Remember how, in previous chapters, I've claimed that without health there's no life? Well, this also includes mental health, both the patient's as well as the rest of the family's. If you don't take care of it, all of that stress and pain can end up exploding in an unexpected crisis. That's what happened to us: My husband exploded on the inside.

At first, we experienced hellish levels of stress over Jon Marcos's illness because we didn't know what to expect. The lack of information, the desperation we felt upon seeing our son in a mental state so despairing that he wanted to take his life . . . I can't even begin to explain all the emotions that stirred up inside. There is no greater pain for parents than the pain of watching a child suffer. If something happens to your child, if you lose your child, nothing else matters. The accumulation of these incidents with Jon Marcos caused Marcos to reach his breaking point during a family vacation to Disney in the fall of 2008.

During that trip, Marcos noticed he had a swollen lymph node in his neck. He went to the doctor and was told it was a cyst. He then began suffering from pain and blurred vision, so he began to worry. He went to many doctors, but no one was able to give him the right diagnosis. Each one said he had something different and prescribed pills to heal him, but nothing worked.

Meanwhile, the only person within my circle of friends who realized something was up with Marcos was Mario Kreutzberger, a Johnny Carson–type personality on Spanish-language television know as Don Francisco. The day I appeared on a telethon he had organized to help the Haiti hurricane victims, he saw that I was alone. I was never alone; I was always with Marcos. Mario noticed this and asked one of my producers why I had come alone. When he heard what was going on with Marcos, Mario said, "Tell Marcos to see a psychiatrist. The symptoms he's feeling might be due to a nervous breakdown." For me, hearing this was a great relief, and I will be forever grateful to Mario for having the courage to say something. Many outside the entertainment industry think that kindness and generosity don't exist within our world; well, Mario Kreutzberger aka Don Francisco is an example that it does. He's incredible. That gesture he made toward us was extra special, because he later explained that he had experienced very difficult moments in his own life, which was why he could recognize what was happening to Marcos. In this world, if you reveal such intimate details, you are exposing yourself and could get eaten alive. That's why I'm so grateful for his kindness and why I cherish our friendship so much.

Meanwhile, Marcos returned to his primary care physician, whom he'd been seeing all his life, and they started from scratch. That doctor took Marcos off all the drugs the other physicians had prescribed, ran the necessary tests, and concluded that the physical symptoms he'd been having were psychosomatic. He sent Marcos to a psychologist. And when Marcos went, the psychologist immediately told him that, given his symptoms, Marcos should see a psychiatrist. When Marcos finally sat down with the psychiatrist, that doctor said, "I don't normally do this, but you have to start taking medication right away." This doctor usually sees his patients at least twice before prescribing medication. That's how bad Marcos's case was.

Jon Marcos's illness had affected Marcos so much that his body and mind were unable to handle the constant state of stress. He remained on the medication and attended regular therapy sessions for a year to help him deal with his depression and nervous breakdown. With the help he received, Marcos was able to feel better, to slowly come off the medication, and conclude his therapy. Crises such as this one often result from dealing with a traumatic experience and should never be ignored; they can affect every aspect of your life. In the end, the psychiatrist advised that everyone in our family had to come to terms with the fact that Jon Marcos may never be 100 percent better, and encouraged us to seek support so we could accept that.

Hope Is the Last Thing to Die

We've been dealing with this diagnosis for eight years now. It began when Jon Marcos was nineteen and now he's twenty-seven. To put this into context, while we were dealing with our shows airing and then being canceled on both Univision and Telemundo, we were also deep in the middle of this huge family crisis. One never knows what another person is going through at home; that's why it's so important to treat one another with kindness and respect. If this experience didn't humble me, I don't know what will.

We've suffered immensely. As a parent, you'd rather have things happen to you instead of to your children. Your nerves are constantly on edge. Jon Marcos went through many stages, but he's much better now. He's such a great cook that every now and then I tell him he should become a chef. He's actually great at a lot of things, but it's still hard for him to leave the house because he doesn't enjoy seeing people. He's still dealing with his bipolar disorder, but he's doing well. He has been back at home with us for the past two years and that makes us happy. We needed to have him nearby. We thought it would be good to have him here with us instead of him being alone at a hospital, where there were no further signs of improvement. We have a team of psychiatrists and psychologists here in Miami who help him, and I believe the love we can give him under the same roof has an enormous healing power.

If you have a family member whose mental health is in jeopardy, always keep the following in mind: Doctors can provide therapy and medicine, but they can't give love. That can come only from family and friends. We surround Jon Marcos with love on a daily basis. He will have to take a cocktail of medications for the rest of his life, but we want him to learn how to be independent because Marcos and I won't be around forever. We want to know that our son can survive without us.

> *There isn't a truer statement than "Hope never dies."*

Never lose hope. Believe me, there isn't a truer statement than "Hope never dies." Those who don't believe in this phrase have probably never experienced a traumatic event in their lives. In order not to lose hope, first you have to hit rock bottom. When you hit rock bottom, when you're drowning in the deepest, darkest depths, that's when you realize the only way out is up. But you have to scrape bottom first to truly understand the meaning of hope.

Today, we have enormous hopes that Jon Marcos is going to be fine. He may not be who he was in the past, but he'll be sufficiently well to take care of himself without us having to constantly worry. My hope shines brighter than ever because my son is taking the right medications and staying in therapy to help him manage his emotional ups and downs. I'm not saying there won't be another crisis, because it's a possibility, but we no longer live in constant fear. We've been through it, we have informed and educated ourselves, and we'll know how to deal with it.

I feel that having Jon Marcos as a son is a blessing. This boy has taught me so many important life lessons, especially that I had not yet learned to be humble. We greatly enjoy his company. We're happy to see his improvement in the last few years, we're optimistic that he'll continue to get better, and we're hopeful that he'll maintain his mental health for a lifetime. We have never lost hope, or the faith that love can help heal a child and a family.

PUT IT TO WORK FOR YOU!

1. Don't be afraid of therapy. If you don't feel emotionally well, get professional help.
2. Don't be ashamed if you or a loved one has a mental disorder. They are very common and, with professional help, can be controlled.
3. Pay attention to your child and loved ones' behavior. If you notice a drastic change in a family member's personality, don't overlook or deny it. Become informed, face the situation, and find professional help.
4. The family of someone suffering from a mental illness must also go to therapy to learn how to deal with the pain and guilt caused by these traumatic situations.
5. Never, ever, ever lose hope.

PART THREE

Life

16

Without Health There Is No Life

Without health there is no life. I mentioned this in chapters 3 and 5, and I want to dive into it here because it's crucial that you understand this concept. Through *The Cristina Show* I learned how important it is to pay attention to your body and take care of your health, and I want you to do the same. You can start by taking these first three steps:

1. Eat a well-balanced diet.
2. Exercise regularly.
3. Visit your doctor for annual checkups.

I'm not a nutritionist or trainer or doctor, so please get professional help if you want to follow a specific diet, exercise routine, or anything that has to do with your and your family's health. In the following pages, you'll find lessons based on my experiences. I hope they will inspire you to take care of your body and health. This should be one of your main goals and one of the basic investments in yourself; don't forget it.

Weighty Issues

Health is essential, and so is accepting your God-given body. Everything is relative in life. When Jennifer Lopez first hit Hollywood, many American women were incredibly jealous; they said she had a big booty and was a little chunky. Yet, despite all that criticism, look at her now. Today, people even get butt implants to look more like her. But that certainly wasn't the case when I was younger. She helped change how the media viewed women physically, and we went from admiring figures such as Twiggy's to yearning for the curves of Jennifer herself or Scarlett Johansson or Sofía Vergara.

It all comes down to your background and where you grew up. The ideal body type varies among cultures, ethnic backgrounds, and countries; therefore, it's essential that you accept the body you were given and focus on what makes you beautiful. For example, I think my butt makes me gorgeous. I also love my legs. I have Basque legs and couldn't have skinny legs even if I wanted to because my body wasn't made that way—and, in any case, I don't like skinny legs. When I used to run, they were super strong and I loved that. Feeling good about your body—and having others perceive you as attractive—is all about confidence and attitude. Focus on what you like about your body and flaunt what you've got; that's what makes each of us unique.

If you think you're a few pounds overweight, first and foremost, find out what your ideal weight is based on your height. Many times, women have an ideal weight in mind that is a far cry from reality. You can't use magazine photos as your point of reference; most of them have been Photoshopped and don't re-

SHARING THE TRUTH

Maintaining a healthy weight, rather than obsessing with every ounce your body weighs, is not only important to your general health, but also to your goals. If you obsess over your weight, you'll spend your days staring down at the scale instead of looking up and living your life. Yes, maintain a healthy weight, eat a balanced diet, drink water, and exercise, but don't let the scale be the center of your world, because if it is, what will all of your efforts and dreams be focused on? Losing weight? If you're focused only on that, you won't be able to concentrate on something far more important: the wonderful life in your hands. So, maintain a healthy weight, but don't let that goal overshadow the rest.

flect reality. Eating disorders such as anorexia, bulimia, and obesity can severely impact your health, so please find out what your ideal weight should be before you take any steps to shed pounds.

Once you've found the weight range related to your height, check to see if you're within that range or not. If you're way below or above it, seek professional help. If you have to lose only

Knowledge Is Power

You can calculate your healthy weight by discovering your body mass index (BMI), a measurement used to associate an individual's weight and height. To calculate your BMI and learn more, visit the National Heart, Blood, and Lung Institute's Web site: www.nhlbi.nih.gov/guidelines/ obesity/BMI/bmicalc.htm.

a few pounds to be within the healthy range, eat a balanced diet and learn more about portion control. But please be careful with any fad diets, because they usually don't have long-lasting results and can even harm your health. There are many diets out there, and if they're balanced, they will work; however, the key to seeing results is to stay motivated and disciplined. You won't get very far if you don't.

The other essential element for weight loss is exercise. Actually, let me rephrase that: Exercise is not only essential for weight loss, it's essential to maintain a healthy lifestyle. I don't want you to obsess over your

> *Exercise is not only essential for weight loss, it's essential to maintain a healthy lifestyle.*

weight. I want you to lead a healthy, active life because that's another important secret to success.

Add Exercise to Your Life

When I started working in television, I immediately found out how important it was to take care of my health and weight. Clearly it's a visual medium, so it's important to look good. I was somewhat unkempt before my television days. After having my children, like many women I continued wearing maternity clothes for a full year until I slowly lost my baby weight. I didn't pay attention to my weight or do regular exercise, and didn't really care about how I looked. There were no overweight people in my family and my body was naturally athletic and muscular. I remember my friends used to call and ask if I wanted to go running with them. Run? No way. I didn't think that was important.

But when I switched jobs and started working in television, my priorities had to change if I was going to successfully adapt to my new career. You've got to feel and look good in a visual medium like TV, because having to deal with a few extra pounds in public is much more difficult; not only do your husband and family say what they think, everyone else does, too.

However, none of the executives actually approached me to demand I lose weight. They aren't that specific, but in the Latino world, since many viewers tune in to check out the women hosting the shows, the executives encourage them to dress and do their hair following the prototype that sells these programs: They've got to be thin, have long hair with extensions, and dress to show some leg. That's why the women on Spanish-language television shows all look the same, and that's why I think it's so important to find your own image to stand out from the crowd, be it in this industry or in any other. To top it off, the executives make these women sit on tall stools and ask them to cross their bare legs to show them off. They even cut out desks on set so that they can show off their legs. In this particular world, diet and exercise are crucial in order to look good on screen.

But I was different. Miguel, my makeup artist, said to me today, "You were the hardest person to convince to wear false eyelashes." I didn't want to wear them because I couldn't read the prompter with those huge eyelashes. I couldn't stand lip gloss because it made me feel uncomfortable when I talked. I felt my lips were stuck together. As I used to explain to Miguel, "The most important thing I do is think and talk." I've had guests on my show who were so swollen from collagen injections in their lips and wore so much lip gloss that I never knew how they even managed to say a word.

Nevertheless, I realized that in order to succeed in this business I would have to abide by certain rules without losing my individuality. I understood this, and that's why I lost weight and let Miguel put those false eyelashes on me. That's also why I paid attention to the focus groups who evaluated how I looked and sounded on the show.

As I was adapting to this new career and the changes in my life, I once asked Gloria Estefan, "Why is exercise so important to you?" And she replied, "Well, when you stand on a stage, it's important not to be overweight. You have sixty thousand pairs of eyes staring at you. You've got to look good."

That's when it clicked, and at forty-one I decided to add exercise to my life. What worked best for me and what I loved most was running. I'd go on three-to-five-mile runs four times a week, every week. It not only made me feel good about my body, it also gave me some time alone, and that was priceless. Now, with the aches and pains that come with aging, I can no longer run, but I still do other types of exercise. You must incorporate exercise into your life until it becomes a part of your daily routine, like eating, showering, and sleeping.

> *Incorporate exercise into your life until it becomes a part of your daily routine, like eating, showering, and sleeping.*

We Must Fight Childhood Obesity

Prevention is one of the basic ingredients for a healthy life. If your body is healthy, you will likely lead a longer, healthier life. Therefore, fighting childhood obesity is crucial in our world today. If you're an obese girl, you will probably have to battle weight issues forever, and that will distract you from achieving your goals. Also, being obese both as a child and as an adult makes you want to hide from the world because you feel insecure about the way you look. This not only negatively impacts your social life, but may stop you from reaching your dreams. Fear of showing yourself in public can lead to lost opportunities during activities or events where you could potentially make new friends, build your professional network, and reach your career goals.

Plus, let's be honest. Society discriminates against overweight people. If you're obese as a child, the crucial time when you should be developing your self-esteem and self-confidence, you will likely have to battle that feeling of being left out due to not participating in social activities the rest of your life— unless you have an extremely strong personality, which is not the case for most people. Do you really want that for your children?

Whenever obese children were invited onto my show, the mothers complained and said, "Cristina, what should I do? See what my child looks like. What a shame." And I would reply, "Have you looked at yourself in the mirror? Do you think this child works, goes to the supermarket, and buys what's in the refrigerator? Give him water instead of sodas and juices, which contain too much sugar." Actually, when I began working for Nestlé Pure Life Water, one of the soda companies got angry with me and called Nestlé's president, requesting that I stop saying their beverages had fourteen tablespoons of sugar per can. But it's the truth! And if we don't communicate the truth, how will we fight the childhood obesity that plagues our children and leads to other serious illnesses, such as diabetes and heart disease?

Knowledge Is Power

According to the Centers for Disease Control and Prevention, U.S. childhood obesity has doubled in children and quadrupled in teenagers over the last thirty years. Children and teenagers who are obese are more likely to become obese as adults and are at risk for health issues, such as Type 2 diabetes, heart problems, and more. If you want to learn more about childhood obesity and how to prevent and fight it, you can start by checking First Lady Michelle Obama's Let's Move campaign: www.letsmove.gov.

Given all this information, I've been involved in campaigns that help fight childhood obesity for a while, the last one being with First Lady Michelle Obama and the Partnership for a Healthier America, where we emphasize the need to drink more water. As a society, we must stay informed and give children the chance to lead healthy, happy lives by teaching them to eat right and stay fit. I completely understand that most parents work hard and don't have time to make elaborate home-cooked meals, so they resort to the easiest solutions in the kitchen. If you're one of these parents, then at the very least please stay away from fast food. Find easier and healthier alternatives for you and your family—add more water, vegetables, and fruit to your daily meals and cross all processed foods off your shopping list.

Physical activity is also crucial for children. Today, most kids spend hours on end playing games on their computers or tablets or watching TV. Set time limits for these activities and make them play outside. My grandchildren, for example, watch TV, but not all day. They stay busy with swimming, karate, and school sports. Find out what sport or activity your child enjoys and encourage him or her to do it regularly. With some simple modifications, you can make huge and long-lasting changes in your children's lives.

The Body Changes with Age

When I was close to forty, I learned how important it was to lead a healthy lifestyle with a balanced diet and regular exercise. Now, at sixty-six, I know that your weight, shape, and the type of exercise you can do will change as you age. And it's also important that you understand and accept this. I don't expect to have the body I had when I was thirty, but I do expect to look good and stay healthy.

Losing weight for TV, for my public image, is quite different from the reason I have to maintain a healthy weight today. Why is it important for me not to weigh two hundred pounds today, if I'm no longer appearing on television? Because my knees won't work at two hundred pounds. If I'm overweight, I can't walk. It's that simple. Having a few extra pounds is harder as you grow older—much harder. As a young woman, through diet and exercise I could easily lose ten pounds in a week. Now, losing ten pounds takes much greater effort and time.

The reality is that with age, you will tend to gain weight. Nothing can stop that. Many recommend that you go to the gym and do a ton of exercise and follow crazy diets to try to stop the passing of time and regain your youthful figure. But that will be the death of you. You have to accept your body and the changes that come with age, and adapt your eating habits and exercise routines to the physical capabilities within your reach today.

> *You have to accept your body and the changes that come with age.*

I can no longer run because my knees and hips can't take it, so I had to find alternatives to continue exercising. I don't expect to have a young woman's figure. What I want is to be happy with who I am and how I look today. Take, for example, Celia Cruz. She was never overweight as a young woman, but as she aged she also added a few pounds. Instead of rebelling against this change, she accepted it as part of growing older, went out and bought some African tunics, and looked and felt amazing. And when her hair began to fall out, she started wearing fantastic wigs and couldn't care less. She felt like a million bucks; she was happy. That's the secret.

To feel like a million bucks, you not only have to accept the limits that come with a particular stage in your life. You also have to take care of your health and adapt your lifestyle to the aches and pains that come with aging, so they don't rule your life. We'll explore this further in the next chapter, but what I want to emphasize now is that you must pay attention to your body, always, no matter what your life stage is at the moment.

At seven, I discovered I had arthritis. I had terrible leg pains, but my mom said they were growing pains—a very Latina thing to say. The only way I could alleviate the pain was by taking two aspirins and tying my sweaters around my legs, which provided some pain-relieving heat. That was the start of my osteoarthritis, which at the time I didn't even know existed. In those days, in Cuba, a relative gave you your diagnosis—"You're rheumatic, just like your grandmother"—and that was it. So I've been dealing with this arthritis my entire life. My daughter Titi also has it, and she runs marathons. But at my age, it's more advanced and I must take the necessary precautions, such as physical therapy, to stay healthy.

That's why it's important to pay attention to what your body is trying to tell you. Titi has arthritis but takes care of her body so that she is able to run marathons. I do physical therapy, among other things, to fight the pain. We must all listen to our bodies and stay healthy according to our particular stages in life. The secret is to be satisfied with who you are and to try to stay as healthy as possible without turning it into an obsession, so that you can continue growing spiritually and mentally.

PUT IT TO WORK FOR YOU!

1. Accepting the body you were given is an essential step in having a healthy self-image.
2. Find out your healthy weight, and if you aren't within that range, take the necessary steps to lose the extra pounds.
3. Incorporate exercise into your life so that it becomes as important in your daily routine as eating and sleeping.
4. Limit the number of hours your children spend in front of a screen and encourage them to be active. If you add physical activity to a balanced diet, you'll likely be able to help prevent childhood obesity, a fate too many children face today.
5. Accept your age and adapt your diet and exercise routines to your present physical needs. The secret is to maintain a healthy lifestyle while you continue to focus on growing spiritually and mentally.

17

*Make Peace with
Your Age and Be Happy*

All of us experience new ailments as we age. The problem
is that we often don't talk about what's going on. My
mom, for example, blatantly told me she'd never gone
through menopause, and my dad took the fact that my mom had
Alzheimer's to his grave without telling anyone else in our family. We have to air these secrets and speak to each other openly
and frankly. We're all going to grow old; that's part of life. Why
not establish an open dialogue about what we experience as we
age, so we can learn from one another?

I want to treat this chapter as a necessary conversation. In
addition to sharing my secrets and advice on how to accept this
stage in your life, I will also reveal certain age-related illnesses
that I've either had to face on a personal level or with a family
member. It's important that everyone absorb this information,
because these age-induced changes not only need to be acknowl-
edged, accepted, and supported by the person experiencing the
changes, but also by that person's family members, since they
will eventually become caregivers—just like I was with my

mother. Whether you like it or not, these changes will knock on your door, so it's best to be prepared for what's coming in order to gracefully and peacefully accept it.

Aging Is Part of Life

I have a friend who's constantly saying, "Ah, I'm fat, I'm fat." And I tell him, "You're not fat, you're old." Aging isn't easy—even less so if you don't know what to expect from this stage in life—but whether you like it or not, this day will come for you, as it does for everyone. The best you can do is understand and accept the changes that occur in our bodies with the passing of time. For instance, you will reach a certain age when your body's fat-to-muscle ratio will not be the same as when you were young, and no matter how much exercise you do, you won't be able to maintain the fat-to-muscle ratio you had at twenty.

> *You have to make peace with what you've become and where you're heading.*

Most of us gain some weight and we all have older bones and muscles—there's no magic pill that will fix this natural aging process. You have to make peace with what you've become and where you're heading.

When Marcos fell in love with me, he always used to say, "Oh, your little intelligent hands. You have intelligent hands," because he hates hands with long nails, and I have a journalist and writer's hands with short nails. However, one day, while I was writing my first book, I stopped and stared at my famous intelligent hands and realized that some bumps were growing on my joints due to the arthritis. I was stunned. My lovely hands were deforming with age. That was my first clear sign that I was entering the dreaded aging stage from which so many people wish to run away, but no one can escape.

However, the superficial changes really didn't affect me that much; what does bother me are the physical changes—in other words, each time I realize my body can no longer perform activities I used to enjoy. The aches and pains that come with age don't only involve dealing with the discomfort they cause; you must also accept that you will have to change some of your habits. Reaching this conclusion and accepting it is one of the hardest steps in the aging process.

A few years back, I wanted to teach my daughter Titi how to water-ski, and that's when I realized that I could no longer do it because I no longer had the required arm strength to pull myself out of the water. I had to accept that I wouldn't be able to teach her one of the things I used to love doing. Those first moments are real eye-openers, because your body is clearly telling you that you can no longer perform a certain activity, but your brain still doesn't understand it, much less want to accept it. I'm still fifteen in my head! Now that I'm at a stage in my life where I finally have time to pick up where I left off with the things I used to love doing before getting into television, like snorkeling, I have to accept that I may not be able to do them because my physical abilities are diminishing. It's the most difficult part of the first stage of aging. But you have no choice other than to face your age-related changes and ailments.

We're all afraid of the changes that come with every stage in life, especially the big changes that define who you think you

SHARING THE TRUTH

People don't know that when I laugh, I pee myself. Everyone reaches an age where laughing means peeing themselves. But no one talks about it, because everyone wants to pretend they are without flaws. Especially celebrities. They don't pee themselves, have plastic surgery, or suffer any ailments because they're perfect. I've had artists sitting in front of me who have obviously gone under the knife a thousand times or more, and they'd look me straight in the eye and say, "No, Cristina, I was born this way." If we continue promoting this supposedly perfect image, we're spreading a false picture of what it means to age. We must start a dialogue with each other, with our families, and more, so that others can find out that, when you reach a certain age, people pee themselves a little when they burst out laughing . . . it comes with getting older and it's normal. So let's slap on those Depends and keep laughing until the end!

are. You grow accustomed to a job and a routine, and when that job or routine suddenly changes, you find yourself catapulted into a new and unknown chapter, and that can be very difficult. You're breathless and uncertain, thinking, *Now what? How do I deal with this?*

When I turned sixty-five, I realized that the issue wasn't my actual age, but what that number represents. It's the age when everyone is expected to retire from work; it's a time when ailments make you confront your mortality. And what do you do if you're not ready to face these changes? Well, even if you're not ready and these age-related changes scare you silly, all you can

> *Everything has a solution if you're willing to find it.*

do is face them head-on and continue your journey. Rise up and shine! Aging happens to all of us—if we're lucky. You will likely have tons of different aches and pains as you age; however, in the following pages I'm narrowing them down to the three I've experienced so far and how I've managed them. I hope my own examples inform and inspire you to be less afraid during this third stage of your life, because everything has a solution if you're willing to find it.

Arthritis

Everyone has arthritis in my family. I got it when I was seven, although at first my family thought it was just growing pains. My daughter Titi has it, too. It's a manageable disease, but continues to progress and becomes more difficult to deal with as you grow older.

Arthritis affects each person differently. Mine has been a lifelong condition, and as I've grown older, the pain associated with my arthritis has become chronic. You learn how to manage the pain because there's no other option, but it's not an easy journey. Arthritis is an illness that limits your will to dream, to travel, or sometimes even to get up off the couch. When our grandson was born, Stephanie's son, I wasn't able to hop on a plane to meet him because I was suffering an arthritis crisis and I couldn't walk.

Arthritis is an illness that slowly begins to affect more and more of your life. Sometimes I think this disease also played a part in my problem with Univision. There came a time when I could no longer jog down the stairs on set as I usually did, or climb on a motorcycle, or ride a horse—all things I happily did in the past. It really confined me. No one enjoys feeling you're limited from doing what you could before. There have been tough times when I've been worried about my health continuing to decline to a point where I wouldn't be able to keep working or enjoy life, but what could I do? That's the card I had been dealt, and that's what I had to face and accept as part of growing older. I've had some pretty amazing experiences, so I can't complain, yet the following ailment that came knocking on my door was completely new and unexpected—another one of those surprise gifts life doles out and that jabs you in the gut.

Ata . . . What?

"Ataxia." The first time I heard that word, I was as bewildered as you might be. What is that? What do you mean it's hereditary? And I have it? Two years ago, I was diagnosed with ataxia, and that was the opening of yet another chapter of aches and pains in my life. It turns out that my family on both sides carries the genes for ataxia as well as for arthritis, but we didn't even know what ataxia was until the doctors discovered I had it a couple of years ago. Hereditary ataxias are a group of genetic disorders. One of the most common symptoms is a lack of coordination, and one of its triggers is alcohol. That's what caused it to emerge in my body.

My mother, may she rest in peace, was the life of every party. She drank like a sailor and would start singing songs by

Manzanero, *"Esta tarde vi llover, vi gente correr y no estabas tú . . ."* That was my mom. My dad didn't drink because he had ulcers, but with such a joyful wife, obviously all the parties were at home. Aside from this, Spanish customs and culture have been present in my family since I can remember. In Spain, you're served wine with every meal and when you're a child, they give you a glass of wine mixed with water. So, drinking for us is quite different from people in the U.S., where they're legally prohibited from drinking until they're twenty-one years old (which doesn't help, because by the time they hit college, they drown in beer, but that's another story).

In any case, I went from that environment at home to the world of journalists, where drinking alcohol is an everyday occurrence. The one who gets the story wins the day, so after work, we'd head to the bar across the street to celebrate or cry together. Then, as editor in chief in the magazine world, where you have to host clients, alcohol also flows freely. And let's not even get started with the TV world. So alcohol has always been part of my life, and I could drink as much as anyone. The amount of alcohol I've consumed in my life is not an example I'm especially proud to share. I'd like women to follow my good examples, not the bad ones. But everyone learns from their mistakes as well as from their triumphs.

When I stopped working at Univision I was sixty-two years old, and for a short time, I was very depressed, as I've already written about previously in this book. During that period in my life, drinking served as part of my defense mechanism. I didn't know what else to do with my time, so I drank some more. Imagine what it's like for a person who has worked nonstop all her life since she was sixteen to suddenly find herself at home with absolutely nothing to do while the rest of the world heads out to work. To console myself, instead of drinking only on weekends, I drank daily, until something strange started to happen. I began to fall, but I quickly realized it was a balance issue because I also fell in the morning, and I never had a drink before five or six p.m.

I started to fall more and more often, until finally I went to see my arthritis doctor, who's brilliant, to see if he could shed some light on what was happening. He examined me and then made me walk. As he observed my steps, he quickly recommended I see a neurologist. There was something wrong with the way I walked. He said it looked like I might have a gait disorder. The neurologist ordered a brain MRI to see if he could pinpoint what was happening to me.

After the MRI, which helped rule out a tumor, the neurologist wanted to know if I had hit my head during one of my falls. I said no.

When I asked him why he wanted to know if I had hit my head, he explained that there was a chance the fluid in my brain and spine wasn't flowing smoothly, and, if that was the case, I would need surgery to have a ventricular catheter inserted in my brain to fix the problem. He was basically telling me I'd need a cerebral shunt in my brain to avoid the accumulation of cerebrospinal fluid. I was terrified and in tears when I got home. Before undergoing such a procedure, the doctor wanted to check the percentage of cerebrospinal fluid and ordered a second MRI, where they once again measured the fluid in my brain. Thankfully, it turned out I didn't have that ailment after all. While they were at it, they also checked for Alzheimer's and Parkinson's—my Saralegui grandfather had passed away due to the latter—because when I walked, I leaned forward and sped up until I lost my balance and fell to the ground. Each time Marcos noticed me walking faster than normal, he knew what would come next. He'd yell at me to slow down, but many times it was already too late. However, the medical team also discarded Parkinson's from the list. We let out a huge sigh of relief, but the waiting game hadn't ended quite yet.

It took three months to get the final verdict, and in the meantime I felt like I was dying. I also felt like time stood still. When you have to wait a long time for a diagnosis, it's extremely difficult because you're left guessing what could be wrong, and it seems like the life you used to have is suddenly over. Not being able to control how your body moves is exasperating; I couldn't even make love. A situation like this one makes you feel like your life has ended, and that's when you really feel old. And so you think, *That's it? It's over?* While we waited for my diagnosis, Marcos was so afraid I'd fall that he even hopped in the shower with me and bathed me to keep me from tumbling over. Or, if I got up in the middle of the night to go to the bathroom, he'd get up and go with me. That's not a problem anymore. I can take showers on my own and walk without falling over, but only because I accepted that I had to take the necessary measures to get better and stay healthy.

When the verdict finally came in, I was told that I had the hereditary genes for ataxia. Ataxia can affect your speech, vision, gait and balance, and many other things. If you have this gene, one of the triggers can be alcohol. That's what happened to me, but I had no idea that gene ran in the family. My mom drank a lot and never fell, and she'd never had any of these symptoms. Neither had anyone else in my family, until now. That's why this diagnosis took me completely by surprise. I had never even heard of this illness.

Knowledge Is Power

According to the National Ataxia Foundation, the word *ataxia* comes from the Greek words *a taxis*, which means "without order or incoordination." People with ataxia have coordination problems because it affects the cerebellum and parts of the nervous system that control movement and balance.

When I received this piece of news, the first thing I asked the doctor was how it was cured, but he told me ataxia has no cure. You are born with a genetic predilection for this illness. However, he explained that if I stopped drinking, which was my trigger, it would noticeably improve. And, in the meantime, physical therapy would make me feel better. I've been doing physical therapy for eight years now. I first started it for my arthritis, and two years ago, when I discovered I had ataxia and could barely walk, I added more sessions to fight this new illness. Aside from physical therapy, I followed the doctor's other recommendation: I also stopped drinking.

Knowing I had to deal with all this, I took the necessary precautions to stay as healthy as possible, of course, but this was another instance where I had to accept my age. We will all be dealt different cards as we age. What happened to me, which doesn't happen to many people, was a great awakening because the things that I had once considered my beacons, such as ambition and work, were no longer as important as simply being able to walk across a room without falling down. My diagnosis brought with it more life changes. There are times like this when you have to make difficult decisions based on your health. It can be scary, but that's when it's important to be strong—and to know you're not alone.

You have to ask yourself, "What am I going to do with this?" Well, when you fall on your face because of ataxia, you have no choice but to stand up and get help if you want to keep on living instead of plunging into a vegetative state. And that's exactly what I did. This attitude can be applied to everything that happens in our lives, be it cancer, AIDS, the death of a loved one, divorce, or the loss of a job. You can't always control what happens to you in life, but you can control how you deal with it and move on. Either you stay in bed and do nothing, or you get up and find the right help and keep walking. Rise up and shine!

> *You can't always control what happens to you in life, but you can control how you deal with it.*

A Mother with Alzheimer's

The person who noticed that my mom had Alzheimer's was her sister, my Aunt Terina, who came over to our house one day and said, "Mati, I think we need to take your mom to a neurologist." I responded by reminding her that my mom was very bohemian and eccentric. But she insisted, saying, "She's not acting like the mom you've always known. Something's wrong, because she asks me about the same thing nine times, I answer, and she doesn't remember that I already answered." When we took her to the doctor, he confirmed she was not well, and said, "Your mom has advanced Alzheimer's." How could we have missed this? Because Mom got worse when Dad passed away; prior to that, he had always covered up her symptoms and taken care of her.

It turns out my dad knew my mom had Alzheimer's, but said nothing in order to protect her. He actually not only wanted to protect her; he also wanted to protect us. He wanted to keep our family image intact, so that everything would remain the same. We were a happy family; my parents adored each other, and he wanted to keep that illusion alive for us.

If you or a relative has Alzheimer's, you must act. Alzheimer's comes in stages. If you notice a loved one showing symptoms, seek professional help . . . help for the person suffering this illness and also help for the caregiver. It's one of the most devastating diseases both for the one who has it and for the family.

Knowledge Is Power

Alzheimer's doesn't present the same symptoms in every patient, but if you learn more about how it develops, you'll be more likely to identify it in your loved ones. For more information about this and other age-related illnesses, visit the National Institute on Aging's Web site: www.nia.nih.gov.

My mom didn't even want to utter the word "Alzheimer's" because she knew how devastating it was, so instead she nicknamed it "Alz." When you have Alzheimer's, you don't notice much of what you do. For example, since this illness requires twenty-four-hour care, instead of putting my mother in an institution, at first I hired a nurse. But a short time later, my mom fired her. So I hired another one. And she fired her, too. One day, I realized I had hired thirteen different nurses, and Mom had fired them all!

Another difficult moment for both of us was when I had to say, "Mom, give me your driver's license. You can't drive anymore." When she went to the doctor to argue about what I was telling her, she knelt down, crying and begging, "Please, don't do this to me." But imagine someone with advanced Alzheimer's driving around town! She could have forgotten where she was or how to get back home in an instant. Driving equaled independence, and I know that losing her independence probably made my mom even more aware that she was losing herself.

Toward the end of her life, whenever I visited her, she would often ask, "Let's see, which one are you?" And I'd reply, "I'm the first one, the one who made you a mom." Then she'd say, "You look so pretty," and would touch my face and then continue, "You look just like me." Picture it: She said I was pretty and looked like her! She had covered the wall across from her bed with my publicity shots, so despite her illness, she understood that I was not only her daughter, I was also Cristina.

My mom never stopped recognizing people completely, like other Alzheimer's patients. What she had were memory lapses. She came and went. When Marcos visited her, they'd sit and chat, but he could tell when she was experiencing one of those lapses. It was like she'd left the building. She even noticed it and gave herself the space for it to pass. She'd focus on the TV, smoke a cigarette, and when she was back, it was like she had reconnected with reality. She'd pick up the conversation where they had left it by asking the same question she had asked before drifting off, and they'd continue chatting. She didn't lose her mind completely. In the end, Mom died at eighty-four from lung cancer—she'd started smoking with her neighborhood friends when she was nine years old. During those last months, she'd slip her oxygen mask off, put on lipstick, and slip it back on—she never let go of her elegance.

When I first had to face up to my mom's Alzheimer's, one of the things that gave me the most comfort was knowing that I'd worked so hard all my life, and now the money I had earned could help me take care of my parents in their old age, even if they were retired and sick. Many people don't have that option. My dad retired because we were able to provide for him, which he needed. There came a time when he couldn't even drive, so we hired a chauffeur. When my mom's Alzheimer's went from bad to worse, I had the resources to help keep her safe and healthy. Having the chance to take care of your parents when they grow old is a huge luxury; it's like buying the house of your dreams or traveling around the world. When I realized that I was capable of doing this because I had decided to pursue my career, I said, "Dear God, thank you for all of the sacrifices I have made. Thank you for all the moments when I chose to do what was required instead of what I desired; because of that, when the time came, I was able to help them."

Make Peace with Your Age

When I have a problem or something happens to me, the first thing I ask is how can I solve it or fix it. And if I'm told the problem can't be fixed, I don't throw my hands in the air and give up; I find alternatives. What can be done? Can it be improved? Yes? Great, then let's make it better. Never give up, regardless of your ailments or your age. I'm not going to lie: It's not easy. But if there's a solution or something within your reach that can make you feel better, do it.

> *Never give up, regardless of your ailments or your age.*

In my case, the hard part has been accepting this new version of myself. I had always seen myself as a sporty and active person, and now, suddenly, at times I can't even walk straight. Once, while at the doctor's office, I watched three people with walkers pass by and I did a double take. My doctor noticed my reaction and said, "When you got here, you were five minutes away from a walker." The problems that accompany aging and entering this third stage in life are the aches and pains, in other words, the physical ailments. Yet, if you keep a young mind and, above all, maintain your curiosity, if you're willing to discover new things, this stage can also be wonderful.

We have to make peace with the passage of time and the ailments of aging. I don't like change, but life is constantly changing, so we must learn to be flexible. And getting old also has its pros, such as the wisdom that comes with experience. Once, referring to *The Cristina Show*, I said to Marcos, "Why didn't all that happen to me sooner, back when I was younger

and physically more fit for the camera, instead of in my forties?"
And he answered, "Because you had to learn all you learned in
the magazine world and in your travels to have a show that lasted
twenty-one years like it did. You needed that foundation and
sense of wisdom and experience, and in order to get all of these,
you needed time."

He was so right. I can stand here today and calmly say that,
given all my life experiences, I'm not afraid to die. It would be a
sin to be scared of death with the life I've had. You have to make
peace with your age, with getting old, with the changes that
come with time passing, and know that each stage has its magic.
Open your eyes and marvel at it. The best way to not fear death
is to live life intensely, with purpose, and to the fullest.

PUT IT TO WORK FOR YOU!

1. You must understand and accept the changes that come
   with aging.
2. Everything has a solution, if you're willing to find it.
3. If you believe someone in your family has Alzheimer's, seek
   professional help immediately. It isn't something you can
   handle on your own.
4. Never give up, not even with the aches and pains that come
   with age. Each person will have to deal with different ailments: Face them, accept them, and move on.
5. Be flexible. Life is made up of constant change. Make peace
   with your age and be happy.

18

Set Some Time Aside for You

T
o succeed in life, it's very important that you set some time aside only and exclusively for you. Sometimes, you have so much going on in your life that it's difficult to even conceive of the possibility of setting a little bit of time aside for yourself, but you need to rest your mind and recharge your batteries. I'm not talking about taking hours or days on end—although vacations are also necessary—I'm talking about setting aside an hour a day for yourself. Do it during lunch, or if you can't do that, get up an hour earlier, or set aside some "me" time when you get home. If you look for it, you'll find that essential bit of time we all need for ourselves.

Even while I was developing my career, raising my family, and dedicating time to my husband, I always found a moment for myself. Time for yourself is essential, no matter what stage of life you're in, but even more so if you're working nonstop. You have to figure out how to identify and take advantage of those precious free moments, because they are there right in front of your eyes and it's time you can't get back.

Value Your Time and Learn How to Say No

Many women find it hard to say no when someone asks them for something. But you can't take care of everything at once. And, if you don't take care of yourself, no one will do it for you. Guard some free time for yourself. To do this, you'll probably have to say that you can't do one thing or another, but that's okay. I speak from experience.

To be able to have time to myself, to be able to concentrate on the things I've wanted to do with my life, to have at least two minutes of mental rest, I had to learn how to say no. When I worked in the magazine world, I had a boss who constantly piled work on me. And what happened? Since I had my own work to finish, I had to fit the boss's tasks into what little free time I had, such as my lunch hour. Yet, what I most wanted was to use that hour to advance my career and achieve my goals. It was time I could use, for example, to write a speech I wanted to give at the Professional Women's Association that week, or to research my interests and create new goals to further my career. So one day, I just said no. I let my boss know that I couldn't do his work because I needed time to write a speech. I said no for the first time. When I left his office and sat at my desk, I told myself, "I said no and nothing bad happened."

That's right, ladies. Usually, after saying no, you'll see there are no big repercussions. The only real aftermath is that with that "no," you will have set aside some time for

> *Usually, after saying no, you'll see there are no big repercussions.*

you, so use it wisely. Remember, you can't please everyone, and it's not your responsibility to do so, either. You can say no! Nothing serious or negative will come of it. Try it out. And when you do, and you get the time you deserve, don't waste it!

Don't Feel Guilty About Your Alone Time

I'm going to be completely honest with you. When God distributed guilt, I didn't get a piece of that pie. I don't feel guilt. I think one of the reasons I've come this far is because nothing makes me feel guilty. If someone's not happy with what I'm doing, let that person be on his or her way. I know what I want and that's what I go after. To reach this point, I had to learn how to say no and understand that I would never be able to please everyone. Find your happiness. If you're happy, you will radiate good energy, and good energy is contagious. One of the reasons many women are afraid of saying no when they're in over their heads is because they feel guilty. You don't always have to be there for everyone. If you don't take care of yourself, no one else will. And to do so, you have to set some time aside for you in your day and in your life.

We must eliminate guilt from our lives, and to do so, you must be the first to break this vicious cycle at home. The first step is to identify the source of this feeling. Ask yourself questions until you find the root of the problem, and nip it in the bud.

Let me tell you a story of what happened to me with a South American woman who worked as a nanny in our home a while ago. Sometimes, Marcos and I would come home early in

SHARING THE TRUTH

Most women worry about their children, their husbands, and their relatives. We dedicate all of our time to our jobs and families and forget about ourselves. We don't have to do this; we just choose to. But it's not entirely our fault. It's what we learned from example—from our mothers and grandmothers. I chose not to teach my daughters this feeling of pure obligation, and they don't feel guilt either. Sometimes I ask my daughter Titi, who works very hard, "Titi, what are you doing at happy hour with your friends and without your husband?" And she replies, "Mami, it was my time to go to happy hour." She has no problem taking some time off to be with her friends, and her husband stays home with the kids and supports her. As a result, she doesn't feel guilty about setting that time apart and doing what's good for her, and that's a sentiment we should start passing on from generation to generation.

the morning, completely beat. Because when you're taping, sometimes things go wrong and you have to stay and fix the problems, which means crawling home at four a.m., exhausted. The nanny was excellent. She would wait for us and when she heard us come in, she'd come to the door to greet us. Until one day she said:

"Doña Mati, you're not taking care of your children the way you should. I'm raising them for you."

"And where are your children?" I asked, knowing she had five.

"In my country," she replied.

"And who's taking care of them?"

"My mother-in-law," she said.

"Then, don't you realize that you and I are doing exactly the same thing? We're working so our families can eat."

That woman worked with us for twelve years, and with this response, she realized that the guilt she was trying to project on me was actually guilt she felt in her own life. This is exactly why I want you to first identify your guilt and figure out where it stems from. Observe your life and identify what makes you feel guilty and do something about it. For example, if you feel guilty because you work too hard and aren't at home with your kids, remind yourself that you're doing it to give them a better life. That shouldn't make you feel guilty. And then dive deeper into your soul and figure out the origin of this guilt. Does it come from your mother, grandmother, or other relatives? Is it something your husband or friends make you feel? Once you understand the root of this guilt, it will be easier to leave it behind. Yes, you have to sit and think. God gave you a brain; use it. Ask yourself things like: Why am I unhappy today? What's wrong with me? What am I really feeling? Where does this anguish and guilt come from? And guess what, ladies, do you know what you need in order to ask yourself all of these questions? Time, for yourself!

> *God gave you a brain; use it.*

Where's Your Alone Time Hiding?

Okay, we've already established that you must learn how to say no and ditch the guilt you feel about setting aside some time for you. Now the key is finding that time. If you have half an hour or an hour for lunch at work, dedicate it to yourself and not to the company you work for. Use those precious minutes to fulfill some of your needs and desires. If you can't take a lunch hour at work, then maybe you can get up a little earlier in the morning and use those precious moments of silence, while everyone is still asleep, just for you. Or you can set aside a little time at night, once the children are off to bed. It's like everything in life: If you look for it, you will find it.

I use my alone time to rest and create a mental parenthesis. I need to stop thinking about work and my daily worries, even if it's just for a little while each day. I realized how much I needed this time when I was working on my TV show, my magazine, radio, and publicity all at once. "Burned out" couldn't even begin to describe my mental state at the time; I was com-

Knowledge Is Power

Scientific evidence states that when exercising, the brain produces and releases endorphins. And there's proof that endorphins, which flow through your body while running or doing other types of exercise, will help you feel a surge of happiness, reduce stress, improve your self-esteem, and sleep better. Not to mention exercise's physical benefits! If you get moving, you'll feel better, and it's a perfect time to set aside for you.

pletely fried. Some time for myself amid that craziness was crucial to my survival and allowed me to keep moving forward. Meanwhile, one of my priorities was to exercise, and that's where I found the precious alone time I so needed. What I loved to do most was run, so I let my mind run along with my body. I felt that exercise cleansed my body, mind, and soul of all toxins. And I didn't like doing it with other people. It was time for me and me alone.

You can use your time to exercise and let ideas flow through your mind, or you can do even more, like I did. I not only ran, I used that time alone to listen to motivational tapes to develop my inner self and continue growing. As my heart pumped and I started breathing hard, I exercised my mind, too, listening to the great motivators and feeling their words fill me with inspiration. And guess what happened? I'd return to my routine fresh, full of energy, and motivated to finish whatever tasks I had left on my long daily list.

Another key resource to feeling well rested and productive is your vacation time. Every full-time job has a certain number of vacation days. Use them! A vacation doesn't mean going far away and spending a lot of money. Even if you take some time off and stay in your area, what they now call a "staycation," those days of rest are crucial for you to succeed at work and in life. When I started working in the magazine world, I didn't have a penny to my name, so I never used my vacation days. When I finally took a few days off to rest, I understood how beneficial that free time was to other areas of my life. Those days off from work rest your mind and give you the necessary energy to continue moving forward. Also, that space gives you time to think of new ideas, which could lead to creating more goals that will help you achieve your dreams. When I first began taking my vacations, I would use half the time with my family and the other half with just Marcos—the perfect combination.

I already mentioned how you can use your lunch hour, or early mornings before everyone is awake just for yourself. Now let me add one more option: nighttime. Another great time slot to set aside for yourself is right when you go to bed, those final moments before you fall asleep. It's the ideal time to review your day, think about how you feel, and focus on what brings a smile to your face. I use that time to pray, think about my feelings, and ask myself why I feel sad or bothered. It's like a therapy session. That moment at the end of a long day, when your body is relaxed and preparing for sleep, is truly unique and personal. Make it yours.

Another way to identify and seize exclusive times for you is to make sure you're playing a sport, attending a class, or engaging in a hobby you love. Seek out those opportunities and make the most of them.

I love to play video games and make handmade jewelry, for example, so the time I set aside to do these things is time for myself. When I play video games, my mind is completely focused on the game, so my brain actually gets a rest from everything else. And when I make jewelry, concentrating on the beads and colors in front of me helps me tune out my work and family concerns.

What I love about making jewelry is that it also includes another one of my favorite pastimes: geography and history. It's not just about making the piece, but about researching the origin of each stone, its history, where it comes from, how it's related to the zodiac, and where that stone is found in the world. I read books that give me more information on these stones or inspire me with new designs. I also greatly enjoy ordering these stones, receiving them in the mail, and using them. It's a fascinating process and real time just for me, moments or hours when I can focus purely on something that makes me happy and forget about everything else for a while. It makes me feel renewed. As an added bonus, I can then sell the pieces and donate the money to Up with Life, the organization Marcos and I started to help prevent AIDS, putting the final products to good use.

Knowledge Is Power

Arriba la Vida/Up with Life is a foundation Marcos and I created in 1996 to educate, inform, and promote collective awareness to prevent AIDS within the Hispanic community in the United States.

If you don't stop and take a breather, your brain won't stop, and you'll end up burning through all of your energy, ideas, and creativity without a way to replenish them. By doing something else for a while, something you enjoy, a strange transformation takes place within your mind. Time expands, and instead of thinking about the past or worrying about the present and future, you're living in the moment and all of the thoughts that usually weigh on you are, for those moments, banished to the back of your brain. Find that precious space in your day and dedicate that time to yourself. Your body, mind, and spirit will thank you.

PUT IT TO WORK FOR YOU!

1. Value your time and learn how to say no. You'll see that by doing so, the only big consequence will be that you have a little extra time for yourself.

2. If setting aside time for you makes you feel guilty, identify the source of that guilt, face it, and deal with it so you stop feeling guilty. If you don't take care of yourself, no one will.

3. Break the guilt cycle and don't teach this sentiment to your children. You are setting an example for them as they grow up.

4. Find time for you in your day-to-day life, be it before or after work, at lunchtime, while exercising, or during those last few moments before bed.

5. Take the vacation time allotted to you by your job. You'll see that a few days of rest will bring immense good to your entire life.

19

Spirituality Is Grounding

Each of us interprets spirituality in our own way, from praying in church to meditating in a garden, but the important thing is to recognize its importance in your life. I respect each person's faith, even though it might not be the same as mine. Our spiritual beliefs truly serve to ground us and are a wonderful reminder that we must all work toward the greater good. I don't believe spirituality is absolutely necessary to succeed in life, but it most definitely helped me. It stops you from abusing what you and others have. For example, community service—and by this I mean the things you do to help others—can be spiritual. Spirituality, to me, has to do with universality, the feeling that we are one.

I consider myself a spiritual person, not a religious one. I wholeheartedly believe that I shouldn't have to "fear" the divine power that created me. And I understood this at a young age. I don't agree with making someone have faith through fear. If you arrived here, and the galaxies arrived here, and everything else arrived here through the work of a creator, why would that creator want to annihilate you? That's a rigid way of thinking, and I'm far from rigid.

Knowledge Is Power

Spirituality manifests itself in different ways, not only within the walls of a church or a temple, or a mosque. You can connect to your spirituality through other ways too, such as yoga, meditation, or being in touch with nature. How you celebrate your faith is truly a very personal choice. Find whatever brings you peace and makes you feel connected with that greater power that fills your soul.

I don't believe in religion's severity, but I do believe in God, and I think we should all openly connect to the divine power with which we identify most. There's no need for us to impose our faith on others. What matters is being connected to your spirituality, to your faith, and surrounding yourself with positive energy and hope.

> *I don't believe in religion's severity, but I do believe in God.*

Connect with Your Faith

My school years were spent in a convent and I was quickly disappointed by the teachings. That's why, when I was twelve, one day I turned to my dad and told him I had decided I would no longer go to Mass. He was stunned and asked why. My answer was simple and direct: "Because I don't believe in God."

"But, Cristinita, how can you say such a thing? I receive communion every day," he said, still in shock.

"First of all, I'm not you," I said. "And second, I've been surrounded by nuns ever since I started going to school and I've seen all they're capable of. And I don't want to be a nun, Dad. I don't want to go to Mass anymore."

Religion was a great disillusionment for me as a child because I was educated in a Miami convent where I saw a lot of hypocrisy. I was never able to believe in religious dogma again, but I was able to reconcile with my faith and my God. Throughout my life, the important thing to me has been God, not religion. Today, when I feel the need, I'll go to a church not because I feel obliged to attend Sunday Mass, but rather to connect with the peace and spirituality that a church can bestow upon me. And I don't confess my sins to any priest because I confess them to myself. Being at peace with myself is all I need.

Aside from what I experienced at school, I also learned a great deal from my show. I saw all the good that spirituality can bring to someone's life, how your faith can help you achieve important things, and I also observed how religious rigidity can blind its followers. Sometimes, that rigidness doesn't allow people to see what's right in front of them. I don't understand people who believe in a religion that doesn't allow them to listen to other people's points of view because they think theirs is the only right one. I'm immensely bothered by that close-minded, intolerant, religious way of thinking that perpetuates the belief that if you're not like me, then you will go straight to hell—especially because I don't believe in hell.

Connect with your faith without fear. Faith and spirituality must be celebrated; they should be something positive in your life, bringing you peace and happiness, rather than fear and guilt. Your faith should encourage you to treat others the way you want to be treated. Don't live your life through gossip and envy. It's

SHARING THE TRUTH

People sometimes don't dare to conceive spirituality in their own way out of fear of God's repercussions. Before reaching your own conclusions about faith, you must first know that by doing so you will not go to hell. You should first be at peace with your God, knowing He will not punish you for seeking spirituality and that faith should not be based on fear. I'm not afraid of my God; He's pure love.

true, human beings gossip as if it were a sport. It's a very common social act. But it's one thing to exchange light, innocent gossip and it's another to hurt people with what you say.

That is, it seems so simple, it's something we all ought to know, but many of us ignore this fundamental truism: Don't do harm to others because it will come back to bite you. Listen, the harm that I've seen people in the television industry do to entire families to get ahead in their careers is horrible. I don't know how they can sleep at night. Let me say it again: They harm whole families and couldn't care less. Many even enjoy seeing others fail because it means they might be able to advance their own careers. Envy kills all spirituality within. Always do your best to steer clear of this feeling, and if you ever feel envy brewing inside, figure out why. If you identify the source, it's easier to change a negative feeling into a positive one. So, instead of feeling envious of other people's achievements, replace it with admiration and find a way to emulate that success.

I'm not saying that you have to wish the best for those who

hurt you, but definitely don't wish them harm. For those who have done me wrong, I don't wish them good or ill, I simply want them to stay away from me. Energy vampires exist and people with bad vibes exist, and you must keep them far away from your life. Distance yourself, but don't wish anyone harm. Follow your path and make sure you're at peace with yourself. Those who surround and fill themselves with negativity eventually burn their own bridges.

And while you're at it, don't forget to smile at other people, to give thanks or to say hello. These basic acts of kindness convey the goodness of the soul, and that's priceless. Sometimes you may forget to pay a compliment or say something pleasant because you're in too much of a rush. Take the time to stop and give positive words to people throughout your day. You can disarm the most stubborn and bad-humored person with good energy and a smile. And that will come back to you. Everything you put out into the world returns to you.

We must find our own ways to nourish our spirituality. Find whatever makes you feel good, comfortable, and at peace. It could be a place or a moment in your day, whatever makes you feel connected to your soul and your God, where you don't feel fear but rather tranquility. For example, Marcos loves to meditate, while I enjoy praying. If you want to pray, it's important that you learn how. You can't ask your God, your Higher Being, for things and demand to receive them on a specific day or explain how they should be sent. On the con-

> *Find whatever makes you feel good, comfortable, and at peace.*

trary, you must surrender to His or Her magic. Prayers must come from your heart and soul, and not involve material things.

I pray every night before going to bed. I always start by giving thanks to the universe for everything it has given me in life to learn from, especially the things many people consider "bad," because that's where I learn the most important lessons. After giving thanks, I pray for everything. Right now, I'm praying for my foot, which I broke when slipping in the bathroom, so that it heals quickly and will let me work and enjoy my family. I also pray for my son a lot. And I pray extra hard for those who wish me harm and those I know have already done me harm. Never wish anything ill on someone who has done you wrong. That's how I pray. Don't remain angry or resentful, because that will eat you up inside. It's not worth it. It's the renowned karma. If you pray for the people who have done you harm and ask for light, that's what you will receive. The connection with your faith and spirituality is essential to finding your inner peace and clearly visualizing your future.

Visualization

There's a huge difference between praying and visualizing. Praying, as we just discussed, comes from the heart and soul, while visualizing is a mental exercise. To visualize means to create an image in your mind and see in detail what you'd like to achieve. It's a concept that I began practicing as a young woman, before it became a familiar concept to many people, and it has led me to obtain much of what I have today.

One of the habits I have developed over time is to cut out

> *To visualize means to create an image in your mind and see in detail what you'd like to achieve.*

magazine articles and images of the things I'd like to have in my life. This habit began thanks to my work as a magazine editor. As I've previously mentioned, I had to keep up to date with the competitive national and international magazines, and I used them to inspire me for our future issues. Every night when I got home from work, I would sit in bed and begin cutting out articles. Sometimes Titi sat with me and helped, while my ex-husband would lie next to me and look on as I worked. Seeing all of those images and reading those articles opened my mind to the world outside my door. They motivated me, and I began to visualize these things for myself because I longed to have a big life.

When I was still married to him, my ex-husband turned to me one day while I was doing this and said, "Don't you realize that by doing this, you're harming us? We're never going to reach those dreams." And I instantly understood that our relationship was coming to an end, because I did believe that I could achieve what I visualized, and with hard work, endless effort, and visualization, I made it my reality.

You should learn how to visualize not only the things you'd like to have, but also the goals you want to accomplish in life. Visualization comes from the mind, so I recommend that you spare no details regarding what you want. The more specific you are, the better, because then the image of what you desire will be clearer in your mind.

For example, if you want to own your own house, imagine

the size of the house, the number of floors, the outside color, the colors of the interior walls, the garden, the balcony, the neighborhood, and the surroundings. Picture it like a detailed drawing. If you want to increase your self-confidence, if that's what you want to achieve, imagine every area of your life and how that would be positively impacted if you possessed that confidence you yearn to attain. Visualize a self-confident image of yourself doing whatever normally makes you feel scared, and break that barrier in your mind.

To effectively visualize, begin with these basic steps:

1. Set aside a specific moment in your day to visualize what you want, be it a thing or a goal. Visualizing doesn't have to take up too much of your time, but make sure you do it every day.
2. Make sure the image you have in mind is chock-full of details. Try to use all of your senses, not just your vision, but also your sense of smell and hearing, until you reach a point where you feel you are inside that image and experiencing it.
3. Once you've turned every detail into a specific image of what you want, surrender it to the universe so it can work its magic and deliver what you desire.

Knowledge Is Power

You have to honestly believe in visualization for it to work. If you have doubts, find more information online, or at your local bookstore or library. The more you know about this practice, the more you will understand how it works and the more likely you will believe in it. If you don't believe, it won't work, it's that simple. Surrender yourself to this belief.

They say we create our own karma through the energy we expend, and that the energy we put out into the universe will come back to us with the same energetic vibe. No one is perfect, and we all have moments when negative thoughts invade our minds. When this happens, try to identify it as soon as possible and clear your mind of this negative energy. Energy is linked to your spiritual life. If you have faith and hope; you wish people well; and if you're kind, giving, and generous, you will be brimming with positive energy, and that positivity will help you succeed in life. Meditate, pray, visualize, and channel positive energy throughout your body, heart, mind, and soul, and you will see incredible results that far exceed your expectations.

PUT IT TO WORK FOR YOU!

1. Open your mind and soul, and don't let your beliefs or religion's rigidity stop you from accepting that people have different beliefs, which are just as valid as your own.
2. Fearlessly connect with your faith and celebrate your spirituality and that of others.
3. When you pray or meditate, never wish harm on anyone. If you ask for light for those who have hurt you, you will also receive light and inner peace.
4. Visualize in detail what you want in life to make it a reality.
5. Get rid of negative energy and channel positive energy throughout your entire being to attract good things to your life.

20

The Journey Is Far More Important Than the Destination

D uring your personal journey in this world, the best advice I can give is that you open your eyes and remain flexible. Even when you undergo moments where all you want to do is hit pause, you won't be able to. If one thing's certain, it's that life goes on, whether you like it or not. So open your eyes wide and enjoy every stage of your life, because the truth is the destination isn't as important as the journey and how you decide to experience it.

You have no idea what life has in store for you, so you have to be ready for whatever comes your way. Since Marcos loves tennis—so much so that our bulldog's name is Rafael Nadal!— I've learned about the game and realized that life is like a tennis match. You have to keep your eye on the ball in order to anticipate where to run. If you don't open your eyes and remain flexible to the changes that come your way in life, your journey will be all the more difficult. Open up to what's in store for you and get the best out of each moment, whether it's a lesson from a difficult experience or a celebration from an achievement.

The other day, as we watched Serena Williams play a championship, she sprained her ankle and made a painful grimace as it happened. When I broke my foot, I heard *crack*, turned pale, and fainted from the pain. This woman did not faint. She sat down, her trainers slid on socks and an ankle brace to fix her up as best they could, and then she got up and kept playing. That was a powerful moment for me because it perfectly captured my philosophy: In life, one must keep on playing and be ready to receive the ball no matter where it comes from.

> *In life, one must keep on playing and be ready to receive the ball no matter where it comes from.*

And Now What?

The goals and dreams we establish and work so hard to achieve are usually met with the passing of time. Then comes the great unknown: What do you do once you've managed to accomplish what you set out to do at the start of your life journey? What comes after all of the successes have passed? When talking with Marcos about this, he said, "One should do what you're doing now, which is making peace with all you've accomplished."

You must fight for what you believe in. I never thought I would become an example people would follow. Actually, when my career took off, I was focused on trying to maintain control of my own life, maintaining editorial control over my product and doing things my way. If you don't control what's yours and don't push it forward with the passion and gumption that only you can put into it, you leave the door open for someone to step in and move your interests to the sidelines.

In hindsight, I think *The Cristina Show* was successful because we weren't trying to turn me into an example other people should follow; I was too busy fighting for what I believed in and trying to be as honest as possible with my audience. My goal has always been to speak the truth. Television is like a magnifying glass. If you're fake on a show like the one I had, it's not only apparent, it's magnified.

I'm the sort of person who speaks without filters and, although expressing my opinions so publicly has caused many problems, I believe that honesty and my wish to share myself with my audience were what united us for twenty-one years. When a woman shared her story with me, I did the same with my own, the good and the bad. By doing so, my audience and I created a very special connection, and I am eternally grateful for their love and support through the years. What's more, the affection forged during the program was something I often felt in real life. My fans are very respectful. When they approach me, instead of asking for an autograph they ask for a hug or want me to say hi to a relative on their cell phone. And I do it with pleasure because I know that our affection for one another is the product of many years, and it's important to maintain that bond.

It's so important to keep our lines of communication open, because it's the only way to remain connected and keep learning from one another as we continue evolving as human beings. When you're a

> *It's crucial that, as women, we share the truth with one another.*

woman, the message you receive from the outside is that you must be a little doll, always pretty, always made up, always quiet and respectful. Quite the contrary, ladies! It's crucial that, as women, we share the truth with one another. You don't have to be a doll; dolls are made of plastic. You're a person. Live your life. I want to believe in reincarnation, and I won't know if it truly exists until my time comes to experience that moment, so I'm enjoying this life down to the very last drop. I hope you do the same.

> *I'm enjoying this life down to the very last drop. I hope you do the same.*

More and More and More Goals

Now that I've achieved most of my big goals, I hope I haven't given you the impression that I'm going to spend my time only taking care of grandchildren. Don't get me wrong, I adore my grandchildren; but I've still got a lot ahead of me, including new goals and dreams that I hope to accomplish. It's important to keep learning and allowing your curiosity to lead you to experience new things, no matter what your stage of life. Live your life with passion because it's all about the journey. And I still have a ways to go.

In this stage of my life, my goals are to stay healthy, continue enjoying my family, and never lose interest in what I do. I want my brain to be as clear in the future as it is today, and I want to continue acquiring new experiences.

I'm sixty-six years old. I still have many more years of life, and I can't let my ataxia win this battle. That's why my health is my main goal, because it's directly related to being able to enjoy my family. When I started physical therapy, my grandchildren would ask me to sit on the floor and play with them, but I couldn't. I explained that if I sat there, I wouldn't be able to get up, and Abu (Marcos) would have to come help Aba (me) up from the ground. I've said it several times throughout this book and here it goes one last time: Without health, you are nothing. I've never understood this as clearly as I do now. And while we're at it, I'll remind you of another phrase that I've repeated incessantly and that I hope is imprinted on your brain by now: Never give up. I want to continue being healthy so that I can enjoy my family and continue doing what I love.

The reason one of my goals is to not lose interest in what I do is because it has happened before. During my last years on TV, I was already bored to death by having to interview celebrities I didn't care about. Most of them don't want to talk about their personal lives, and those experiences offer the best lessons for the rest of us. I not only want to stay curious and continue learning, I also want to continue sharing information with my audience, so that you, too, can continue learning. If I get bored, you will get bored, too, and that's not the idea.

Now I'm doing radio and, many times, although I enjoy these programs immensely, I miss the camera. When I want to show something to my listeners, I can't, so I describe it instead, which doesn't have the same effect as visual media. After so many years on TV, I've grown so used to showing that Marcos still has to remind me that my audience can't see me on the radio. The truth is, I would love to return to television; I enjoy and miss it, but I would need to do it under certain conditions. When we first started *The Cristina Show*, we focused the programs on social issues, like we do now on my radio show. These topics are what I love to explore and discuss. However, slowly *The Cristina Show* shifted its focus to celebrities, and there came a point where I noticed this and became bored. If I receive a new proposal, it would have to involve something that I am truly passionate about.

Enjoy the Journey

I wouldn't change anything I've done in my life. I consider my life to be an amazing journey, and I still have much more to experience. Additional advice I'd like to leave with women of all ages is that you always be truthful; stay curious, don't be afraid to enjoy and explore new things; and don't abandon your sexuality, because sex is delicious, and whoever says it isn't has no idea what he or she is talking about.

The universe gives us the chance to evolve when we are aware of the messages it bestows upon us. What I have learned throughout my sixty-six years of life is that love is stronger than hate, a smile can be the prelude to a good deed, living with passion is better than just living, and remaining silent if you have nothing good to say is more compassionate than lying.

> *The universe gives us the chance to evolve when we are aware of the messages it bestows upon us.*

Whatever you want to do for yourself, make sure it has a bigger purpose and do it for more reasons than simply personal gain, and, please, make sure it makes you happy along the way. As Marcos so wisely taught me, the journey is far more important than the destination. The truth is, reaching your destination or achieving the goal is probably the easiest step. The journey itself is the real challenge and yet the most essential part of the experience. Try to enjoy the ride and be open-minded. Until the day you die, life will continue to present you with different paths so you can learn from them. And if you haven't learned from the journey, what were you doing?

After everything I've experienced, I've not only been able to make peace with this stage of my life, but also with who I am. In life, as time goes by, you must learn the key difference between doing and being. You can do a ton of things in life, but at the end of the road, you have to be crystal clear about who you are. That was hard work for me, but I know now that media Cristina is only part of what I do, because these days I am Aba, Mami, and Mati, and the happiest moment of my life is the present one.

PUT IT TO WORK FOR YOU!

1. Remain open and flexible to what life has in store for you.
2. Never give up.
3. Face your fears head-on and conquer them.
4. Live your life with honesty.
5. Choose to do what you love and makes you happy, and, please, enjoy the journey.

*Hope is the last
thing to die.*

Acknowledgments

As I mentioned in the book, I once said to Marcos many years ago, "It's too bad I wasn't younger when I started my TV show." In 1989, when *The Cristina Show* made its debut, I was forty-one years old. After a slight pause, Marcos replied, "Mami, you needed all those years of magazine experience in order to do what you do today so well." He was right, because the only thing you can't improvise in this career is experience, and the only thing you must never forget is that many people helped you along the way.

To all of you, thank you for all of the hard work and for the achievements we have accomplished together, because although I was the face of it all, this has always been a team effort.

Among my many colleagues, I'd like to mention a special man who gave me unconditional support, my executive producer for *The Cristina Show* and all of my TV projects: Mr. Osvaldo Oñoz. Thank you, Ozzy!

To my work son, Jorge Insua, who often believes in me more than I believe in myself. Thanks to his persistence, this book is a reality.

To my brother and personal assistant, Iñaki, thank you for putting up with me. I don't know how you do it.

To Ray Garcia, Celebra publisher, who pursued me for four years to make this book and never gave up. Thank you, my friend.

To Kim Suarez, my editor, whose positive attitude and great management skills never let this project lose its way. Thank you!

To Holly Robinson, thank you for your editorial expertise and for the quality work on the manuscript. I am forever grateful.

To Andrea Montejo, for her sound advice that shed light on the manuscript. Thank you!

To Cecilia Molinari, who sat with me and helped shape this project, you have no idea how much I will miss you now that we are done. Thank you, friend; many, many thanks.

And finally, a heartfelt thanks to my audience and fans for supporting me throughout the years: You've enriched my life in ways you will never know. *¡Los quiero mucho!*

Recommended Reading

The following list includes five books that have changed my life, and I suggest reading them as a way of continuing to learn how to achieve your dreams and be happy. After reading them, I hope you apply their lessons to your journey through this world, so you continue to rise up and shine!

1. *Creative Visualization*, Shakti Gawain (New World Library, San Francisco, 2002)
2. *The Secret*, Rhonda Byrne (Atria Books/Simon & Schuster, New York, 2006)
3. *Seth Speaks: The Eternal Validity of the Soul*, Jane Roberts (New World Library, San Francisco, 1994)
4. *Think and Grow Rich*, Napoleon Hill (The Ballantine Publishing Group, New York, 1987)
5. *The Power of Intention*, Wayne Dyer (Hay House, Carlsbad, 2005)

About the Author

Cristina Saralegui made her television debut as host and executive producer of *The Cristina Show* in 1989 on the Univision Network. The show broke down all barriers and became a television success. For twenty-one years, Cristina and *The Cristina Show* entertained, uplifted, and educated the Hispanic community in the United States and throughout the world, and became the platform and voice for millions of Hispanics who may not have otherwise been heard. This Cuban-born media mogul was chosen by *Time* magazine as one of the "25 Most Influential Hispanics in America" and is the first Spanish-language television personality to receive a star on the Hollywood Walk of Fame. Additionally, she has received numerous awards, including twelve Emmys, the Foundation of American Women in Radio and Television's Gracie Allen Tribute Award, amfAR's National Community Service Award, the Simon Wiesenthal Center's 2004 International Distinguished Achievement Award, as well as The Hispanic Heritage Foundation's Arts Award and the Imagen Foundation's Lifetime Achievement Award. Cristina is the first Latina to be inducted into the Broadcasting & Cable Hall of Fame, where she joins such television legends as Walter Cronkite, Barbara Walters, and Johnny Carson.

For more information, follow Cristina on Facebook at www.facebook.com/CristinaSaralegui or on Twitter: @CristinaOpina.